FRIENDS IN LOW PLACES

FRIENDS IN LOW PLACES

Testimony of a Muslim Who Found Jesus and a Mission in the Bronx

Habib Ibrahim, MD

iUniverse, Inc.
Bloomington

Friends in Low Places
Testimony of a Muslim Who Found Jesus and a Mission in the Bronx.

iUniverse books may be ordered through booksellers or by contacting:

iUniverse
1663 Liberty Drive
Bloomington, IN 47403
www.iuniverse.com
1-800-Authors (1-800-288-4677)

ISBN: 978-1-4502-9002-9 (sc)
ISBN: 978-1-4502-9003-6 (hc)
ISBN: 978-1-4502-9004-3 (e)

Library of Congress Control Number: 2011908510

Printed in the United States of America

iUniverse rev. date: 06/27/2011

Contents

To my sparring partner and wife, Anne.

I would like to dedicate this book to Anne, my lovely wife of twenty-five years. I consider my wife to be my sparring partner; she is training me to take on the challenges of working in the mean streets of the Bronx. Muhammad Ali's sparring partner was Larry Holmes; mine is Sugar Ray Anne. To my wife, I am her Hurricane Habiby. My wife toughens and inspires me by telling me *just how stupid this book is*: "What? You're going to tell your readers what some crack addict at our clinic said, 'Bronx love is the best love'? Why don't you tell them about Christian love instead? And turn down that reggae music!"

CHAPTER 1

The Parable of the Perfect Teapot

Twelve years ago, I found Jesus, and I found my calling. I am on a mission to bring God's love and healing to the Bronx, and in so doing, I seek God to do good work in me—to purify my spirit and reveal His purpose in my life. This book also contains the testimonies of other people who found the love of Jesus, including the following: two Muslims—one a tank driver in the Afghani Army during the Russian occupation; a gangster; a crack cocaine addict; and an Orthodox Jew.

As a physician who has treated HIV for more than twenty years, I have always tried to find better solutions to bring medical care to the most disenfranchised people in the Bronx. The best solution came to me in a dream while I was still a Muslim (see chapter 4). I saw Jesus motioning with his hands, saying, "Bring them to me, and I will heal them." Upon awakening, I could feel the love of God, and I had a new passion to bring God's love and healing to the Bronx. I became a partner in a clinic where none other than Jesus Christ served as the Master Physician. In yet another dream, I saw Jesus walking through the poorly lit, narrow hallway of the clinic, bringing light to each of the four examining rooms as he blessed our HIV patients.

Christ's message was one of love and reconciliation, and that message is the underlying theme of this book. My favorite Bronxism, spoken by a crack cocaine addict, attests that *great burden* brings out *greater love.* He said, "The Bronx love is the best love." Through our troubles and suffering, God permits the water of life to come to a boil, and the Holy Spirit provides the tea leaves, with which we are to flavor our lives. When the tea is brewed and ready, God Himself will pour the perfect tea from the perfect teapot, into the sinless cup. The cup is the sacrifice of Jesus. And finally, God will take a long, satisfying sip for His pleasure.

Join me on a fifteen-year spiritual journey in search of the perfect teapot. The teapot is not far, for it is *your heart.* The purpose of the journey is to brew the best tea, or to create a human spirit that best reflects the Holy Spirit of God. The journey of life is not measured in miles, but rather by milestones: becoming a believer in God (chapters 7 and 8), finding the love of Jesus (chapter 4), finding God's purpose for your life (chapter 3), finding the place where God wants you to serve (chapter 2), finding a spouse who brings out the best in you (chapters 5 and 6), having fun (chapter 9), coping with rebellious children (chapter 10), challenging sickness (chapter 11), growing old, and finally dying with dignity (chapter 12).

God cares little about our destination; for Him, it is a short distance to our perfected hearts. He knows our spiritual potential while we persistently ask, "Are we there, yet?" God is only concerned about whom we bring along for the trip, and how we compose ourselves during what seems a long journey. God wants His children to "Play nicely in the backseat." God is not a respecter of human institutions, politics, socioeconomic class, religiosity, intelligence, or our selfish desires. When the journey is over, and we leave this world to stand before God, He will ask, "Did you visit me in the hospital, did you visit me in the jail, and did you visit me in the orphanage?" God identifies Himself with the meek, the lowly, and the unfortunate crowd, and God wants everyone in a "high place" to stop being arrogant and reconcile with the "lowly" crowd. He will ask us just one more thing, "Did you leave behind a legacy of love and reconciliation?" Nothing else we do matters to God.

The principle of reconciliation through unconditional love holds true for all people and in all relationships. In the relationship between warring nations, this principle brings *peace*; in the relationship between squabbling family members, this principle brings *harmony*; in the relationship between a sinful individual and God, this principle brings *joy*.

My oldest son, Anwar, enjoys drinking tea. He is somewhat of a tea fanatic. One day, while we were drinking a cup of monkey-picked, oolong tea, my son told me the story of his search for the perfect teapot. Anwar had been shopping at an upscale store for a teapot. He asked the salesclerk for a teapot that perfectly reflected a tea reality where East meets West, high meets low, and old meets new. The salesclerk was delighted with my son's request, as if the clerk had been waiting all his life for someone to come along and ask for this particular teapot. After a momentary search in a dusty, old storage room, the salesclerk emerged with his prize—a very inexpensive, used teapot. It was handy and small, with only enough water space for two cups. There was nothing ornate about the pottery, nor was there any indication of where it was from, not necessarily from the East, nor from the West. It only came in one of five colors: black, white, brown, red, and yellow. It was neither rustic nor was it modern in design—the potter who had created it was very pragmatic, as if the only consideration was to design a pot that would brew the best tea.

I pondered the significance of my son's "tea reality," and I believe it speaks of a journey that epitomizes the entire contents of this book. The journey is to brew only the best tea, or if we crack the code of the analogy, to create a human spirit that best reflects the Holy Spirit of God. God is the pragmatic potter. The teapot represents the hearts of all humanity, seen in one of five basic skin tones. The salesclerk is our spiritual guide. My son is a seeker of God.

There is an old Sufi Muslim saying for those who seek God: "Oh, you who thirst for the tea, you do not realize that the tea also thirsts for you." Without God and His plan to let us drink from His Spirit, we would surely remain thirsty. In John 3:16, Jesus was the ultimate spiritual guide, but Jesus was more than just a spiritual guide; it was God's loving plan to use the sacrifice of Jesus on the cross to provide a sinless cup for those who are thirsty. It was God's plan to make perfect the human spirit so that God can love us perfectly, because God also thirsts for us.

Now that I have turned fifty, I feel as if *I am* that used teapot (what good is a teapot if it is not used?)—middle aged, not young, yet not ready for the grave. For my first thirty-eight years, I was raised a Sufi Muslim, a kind of born-again Muslim, and a seeker of God. I continue to seek Him, but for the last twelve years, I have taken Jesus as my guide, my teacher, and my savior. My profession is as an internal medicine doctor whose specialty is the treatment of HIV. My clinic is in the Bronx, New York City, serving my *friends in low places*.

God loves all people equally: the smart and the stupid, the beautiful and the ugly, the young and the old, the male and the female, the Republican and the Democrat, the healthy and the sick, the perfumed and the malodorous, the Yankees and the Mets, the atheist and the believer, all the children of Abraham—Muslims, Christians, Jews—and everyone else.

There is nothing we can do to make God love us a little more or a little less. God sent Jesus to identify with people, even those in *low places*, hence the title of this book. Of course, from God's perspective, we are all in a *low place* and in need of His saving grace. God sent Jesus to love the unlovable and to touch the untouchable. Jesus ministered to those who were despised and cast out of society: the tax collector, the prostitute, those with leprosy, the lame, the blind, and the downtrodden. When his opponents accused Jesus of mingling with the wrong crowd, Jesus responded, "Does not a doctor keep company with the sick?" I am gratified that sometimes God likes to play doctor, because we doctors sometimes like to play God.

Join me on a humorous, sometimes poignant, walk through my life, from age thirty-five to fifty. Through the trials and tribulations of life, we strengthen our faith and perfect our spirit—all for God's pleasure. My wife warned me that this book could get me in trouble with fundamentalist Muslims, puritanical Christians, Jews, Quakers, atheists, Mets fans, the French, and even feminists. I am not sure who I should fear the most—the Hamas, the feminists, French girls, or just anyone with hairy legs. Maybe I will be beaten up by a bunch of Quakers. Please note that I do not mean to be irreverent to anyone's sensitivities or religious beliefs. Leave your fatwas of death, your excommunications, your circumcisions, and your TSA airport security checks at the door, please.

This book will show you how to reconcile things that are very different, so that it will seem easier to reconcile things that are nearly the same.

Described in chapters of this book are the competing dichotomies that are most in need of reconciliation:

1. Arabs meet Jews.
2. You meet the place where God wants you to be.
3. You meet the Godly purpose in your life.
4. The sinner meets Jesus.
5. Male meets female.
6. Body odor meets perfume in a subcompact Smart Car.
7. Atheist meets believer.
8. Islam meets Judeo-Christianity.
9. The Yankees meet the Mets.
10. Old meets young.
11. Health meets sickness.
12. Aging meets fear of dying.

There is a thread of God's decency, sanity, and love in all people—no matter how confused they may seem. This book celebrates that thread and attempts to fix many fouled-up relationships. For example, Jews and Arabs are nearly the same, they are both Semites, but they fight one another ferociously. Instead, they should focus on reconciling relationships with their rebellious, hormonally challenged teenagers, who plague all parents. Instead of fighting over the Gaza Strip, Aaron will say to Ahmed, "Hey, Ahmed! Just when we think that we've finally humanized our children and we can live with them, they go and live with someone else!" Ahmed will reply in a thick Middle Eastern accent, "Yes, Aaron, you're right! I call that *'gonadal thinking.'* Instead of their brains, *they think with their gonads*, and they only think *about their gonads*. The love of God is greater than our differences!"

Love will rule the day when Jews and Arabs find that they have a common enemy—young adults with raging testosterone and estrogen.

What is the solution to the conflict in the Middle East? I figured it out during a wedding of a Jewish friend of mine. It is this: there should be a law that forces Israelis to go to the weddings of Palestinians, and

Palestinians to go to the weddings of Israelis. Peace will come when both sides see how beautiful and full of hope the bride is on her special day and how everyone loves the Chicken Dance. Imagine if hundreds of young Palestinians and young Israelis who met at such weddings married and started having kids. That would screw up the hateful theology of politicians on both sides. Imagine the awkwardness of Ahmed, the suicide bomber who is supposed to kill some Israelis, when he recognizes Aaron from the wedding he attended last month. What's he going to say? "Hey, aren't you Aaron from the Israeli wedding? Lovely bride! Any children? No, not yet? I'm sorry, but I have to blow us up now, okay?" That would be ridiculous. Killing cannot happen when the parties involved are humanized to one another, such as through a wedding. **(Bronxism: God don't like ugly.)** What is ugly? It is unfairness, injustice, and cruelty *just for the sake of* unfairness, injustice, and cruelty.

The Christian world is clamoring for moderate Muslims to denounce the actions of fundamentalist Muslims. People like me are the answer to that request—you cannot be any more moderate than a Muslim who has embraced Christ. I have some strong words for the fundamentalists in chapter 8. I call myself a Christian, but *all I really want is Christ*. I do not want the institution of Christianity. I do not want organized religion with all its rules and regulations. I want to know God. I want to sip the tea of His Holy Spirit, to feel His love, to be in His presence, to hear His wisdom, to obey His commandments, and to serve His creation. I will humbly take anyone's advice that can help me to know God—whatever his or her religious background, color, age, or socioeconomic standing.

On the other side of the coin, the Muslim world is clamoring for democracy—just look at Tunisia, Egypt, Libya, and other Middle Eastern countries. What these people really crave is the love of Jesus Christ. Unfortunately, Muslims label evangelical Christianity as a form of American imperialism, peppered with the intolerant ranting of a Florida pastor who burned the Koran. (I won't use his name to protect his life from the radicals.) This pastor had an improbably long mustache, which was likely pasted onto his face. It seems that his mustache was as phony as the man's phony version of Christianity. His church is called the Dove

World Outreach Center, which is a terrible misnomer because his church is slinging hatred with the naive and grandiose belief that hearts would be changed and a better world would be created. In the Bronx they will kill you for a five-dollar metro card, but they will never insult your religious beliefs—that would be the height of ignorance and insanity, or as Will Farrell said in the film *Zoolander*, "What? Are we all on *crazy pills?*"

If the Florida pastor had ever read his Bible, he would have learned (from the book of Romans) that while evangelizing, it is desirable not to become a stumbling block to your audience. This Florida pastor is known to carry a gun for protection, but if he were really led by the Holy Spirit to burn Korans, then God's protection would have been all he needed. Jesus impacted all humanity, for all time, yet Jesus never packed an AK-47. Jesus's only weapon was the cross upon which he was crucified. In Matthew 5:44, Jesus said, "Love your enemies and pray for those who persecute you, that you may be sons of your Father in heaven." See chapter 8 for a story regarding this scripture, "The Torn Page," and how it affected an Afghani soldier who drove a tank during the Russian occupation of Afghanistan.

Jesus and Muhammad said the two most influential sayings of all time, spoken thousands of years ago, and hundreds of years apart, at a time when each man was giving advice to people who feared that death would soon take their spiritual guide away. Muhammad was mounting his horse to go into battle when someone stopped him and asked for a synopsis of Islam, to which Muhammad replied, "Islam is the surrender to Allah, and you must obey Him and serve His creation." The disciples of Jesus became worried after Jesus told them that his mission was soon to lead him to death on a cross. In desperation, one asked him, "Master, what shall we do after you are gone?" Jesus responded with an answer that was as profound as it was simple. He said, "Love one another."

I could be wrong about a number of things; I am not a theologian, thank heaven. This is not a religious book, but it speaks of *the universality of God's love*. The book is a free-flowing, somewhat psychotic representation of things that I have learned in the last fifteen years of my life. There are quips from my Bronx patients, which are often colored with deep meaning—these survival truths are often funnier than fiction. I draw upon testimonies of life: my life (through my essays), my Bronx patients' lives, and the lives of Christians, Muslims, and Jews that I know. I hope that one day I will be invited to talk about this book on Jon Stewart's *Daily Show*, and on Bill O'Reilly's *The O'Reilly Factor*. (*Comedy Central* meets *Fox News*.) God loves the hosts of both shows. The pinnacle of my life would be to have a cup of tea with Jewish comedian Dennis Miller—not just to seek a Kumbaya moment with a Jew, but because he is smart, satirical, and funny.

Life is what happens while we are making other, more complicated plans. Why are we so often blindsided by life? It is probably because we insist that our teapot must be a certain way. Either it should be too old or too new, too ornate or too plain, too much from the East or too much from the West. Another common mistake we make is to pretend that a person, or a group of people with our shared ideology, can love us perfectly—only God loves us perfectly, and we must seek His love before any other. I am grateful that my son Anwar has shared with us his pursuit of the perfect teapot. I'm very proud of Anwar and all my children, and I hope they all stay thirsty for the tea. The potter wants to simplify our lives, and the pot should only serve one purpose: to brew the best tea, the best human spirit.

CHAPTER 2

Meeting the Bronx

I have a love affair with the Bronx. We "keep it real" in the "*boogie-down*" Bronx. I met my wife when I was a medical student at Bronx's Lincoln Hospital, where she was also working. She will tell you that the first time she saw me, God said to her in a baritone voice, "Dr. Ibrahim will be your husband!" That voice was actually me from behind a curtain. I had passed by her and then doubled back. In my best baritone voice, like a Pakistani Barry White, I gave her the epiphany of her dreams. On the other hand, like most men, my earliest attraction to my wife had very little to do with God's calling. I finished my residency at Our Lady of Mercy Medical Center. Our first son, Anwar, was born at Lincoln Hospital. My first private practice clinic was in the Bronx. Then, of course, we have the Yankees!

My clinic is a dangerous place, and for five years, I was both the doctor and the security guard. I decided to hire a security company after a patient choked one of my staff. I had to hold the offender down until the police arrived. Three security companies refused to work in our clinic. The reason they gave: "It is way too dangerous!" It is hard to keep a physician's assistant employed at the clinic, because one was choked, and one almost took a bullet inadvertently in a drive-by shooting. My current physician's assistant is a tough old Catholic guy who is not afraid to see Jesus soon. I do not carry a gun, because I know God has placed me in the Bronx for a purpose. God's will has led me to a place where the grace of God will keep me safe. Guardian angels surround me; these angels represent every gang in the Bronx. My patients look at my Puerto Rican son-in-law-to-be, and my Afro-American daughter-in-law, and ask me if I plan to create the Ibrahim Gang with my grandchildren. To each gangster, and nongangster, to those with and those without HIV, I equally show God's love and give good medical advice. Love is, among other things, a good safety policy. If the Islam-hating, Florida pastor comes to the South Bronx and continues to evangelize without love, then I suggest he get himself a bigger gun. **(Bronxism: what goes around comes around.)**

My most noteworthy evangelical experience in the Bronx was to the king of all gangsters. I'll never forget the first day O. G. (original gangster), one of the three founders of a prominent New York City gang, came to my clinic. O. G. was on death row four times, because he killed more people than he has fingers and toes. The FBI stayed his execution because O. G. pledged to help mediate on behalf of the government with the gangs.

O. G. was having his blood drawn by my four-foot-nine, female medical assistant, and I could hear his loud whimpers and screams coming from the laboratory. It was getting annoying. I mused aloud, as I walked down the hallway to my office, "Who's that crying like a little girl while he's getting his blood drawn?"

The medical assistant brought me the patient and his chart. The chart noted that he was six feet tall, but he seemed taller than life. He had a thin, lanky build—that of a lightweight boxer who could hit you six times before you blinked. His thin, well-groomed mustache with a hint of gray dated him to be about sixty years old. He was immaculately dressed in a suit but no tie. His unbuttoned silk shirt exposed a muscular chest and a gaudy golden chain. His alligator shoes were shiny and made a clicking sound when he walked. This clicking was probably the last thing his victims heard on this side of eternity. He looked at me with a confident stare, apparently sizing me up to see if I could be trusted to be his doctor.

When I see a tough guy, I often like to disarm him with humor. I wanted to break the ice, so I asked him, "Are you the guy who was being molested by my tiny little medical assistant? Do we need to get you someone even smaller to draw your blood?"

He answered my question with a question: "Do you know who I am, and do you know why half of your waiting room just now cleared out?"

I thought that was a strange response, but I was not going to let it stop me from having some fun, so I picked up his chart and read him his name. "I know who you are; it says here on the chart your name is O. *'Little Girl,'* G!"

He appeared taken aback by my boldness. "Say what! No, you really don't know who I am!"

Starting to get a little nervous, I asked sheepishly, "Who are you?"

He stood and got within an inch of my face. "I'm O. G., original gangster, father of the greatest gang in New York!"

I felt all my blood pool at my feet. I offered up these final words to the last person I would see before I died: "Now you're going to see *me* cry like a little girl!"

Fortunately, O. G. had a sense of humor, and since I looked so pathetic, he let out a good belly laugh. I proceeded to tell him about Jesus, not so much to save his soul, but more to save my own life. On that day, O. G. found the love of Christ, I gained a brother, the Bronx became a safer place, and I lived to tell the tale.

I have a few questions for any atheist reading this book: Would you rather be held up by a gangster who is an atheist or one who feels accountable to God? What about a nuclear physicist with the formula for an atomic bomb? (Chapter 7 gives the story of Albert Einstein.) Or what about a doctor wearing rubber gloves on his gigantic hands, an amorous TSA airport security worker, or a pedophile schoolteacher? People have hideous, deranged motives. Why would you not want them to feel accountable to God?

Through O. G.'s and hundreds of others' changed lives, I have seen how the same people who were once opposed to God have been used as agents to execute God's plan. In his own writing, O. G. says, "I was once doing the Harlem shuffle, dancing with the devil, but now I walk with God. I am striving every day to be more and more divinely led. As each day brings more challenges and change, each of us needs to listen closely to what God is trying to tell us about our particular assignment and duty to Him."

From God's perspective, no one should remain lost without love or wisdom. That's why God has made it possible for people at both ends of the faith spectrum to acquire wisdom. The sun shines equally on the wicked and the wise. God's mercy is all-inclusive, and God chastens the one who He is drawing near. A person can learn the same lesson by being opposed to God's will as he can by being compliant with God's will. One route to wisdom is easy and direct; the other route is circuitous and agonizing. Former atheists make great witnesses of God's will. Once the atheist turns to God, he has a strong testimony, because he has graduated from the school of hard knocks. I will illustrate this point with the story of another patient of mine.

I once told one of my crack-addicted AIDS patients, J. R., that I envied him. When he asked why, I told him that he is the one lost sheep God is actively seeking. On the other hand, I am one of the ninety-nine sheep already in the pen. I'm jealous because God has his eye on lost souls, and God is persistently drawing them near to Him. There is again the Sufi saying that speaks of God's thirst for us: "Oh, you who thirst for the tea don't realize that the tea also thirsts for you."

J. R. told me he would always be an atheist. His reasoning was that all his friends who became Christians at the end of a long battle with AIDS had died. I told him that Christians do not fear death because the worst that can happen is that you die and see God. I shared with him accounts of people who have come back to life after a near-death experience. These people often describe God as a warm and loving bright light. These near-death survivors wished they could stay a bit longer with God's light, but it was not their time to die, and they were jolted back into their physical bodies. Death loses its bite for those who have reconciled with God's love in the afterlife. They go on to live without the fear of death, and some actually would welcome death; furthermore, they reorganize their priorities and stop living selfishly. The best thing that I told J. R. was that, although these near-death survivors were sinful people, the few moments they spent in the company of God's light changed them forever.

Despite my invitation, J. R. rejected the knowledge of the love of God. Two months later, he returned to my clinic, emaciated and homeless. It turns out that he was found unconscious in his own urine and feces, and then he was rushed to the hospital. He was hospitalized for a week and treated for cocaine-induced seizures. When he was finally released from the hospital, his apartment had been robbed, and the landlord had kicked him out. Now he was homeless. He said to me, "Doc, I know you're going to say, 'I told you so.'"

I shook my head. "Nope, but I'm going to ask you something else."

J. R. grew curious. "What?"

I looked him right in the eyes and asked, "Can I call you my brother?"

He seemed perplexed. "Why would a fat-cat doctor like you want to call a crackhead like me a brother?"

"Because if we are brothers, then that means we have the same father. God is our father. Why don't you come home to Him?"

J. R. broke down and cried. It had been a long time since anyone had shown him that God was reaching out to him. From that day forward, he became a model patient, gained weight, stopped using drugs, started to attend a local church, and has a strong testimony, which he freely shares with other down-and-out people. His evangelism is out of gratitude for the love of God. Love, especially the unconditional love of God, is the best thing in life.

In the words of Søren Kierkegaard, "To love another person is to help them love God."

On another occasion, I surprised my staff when I ran up to a dirty, smelly homeless man who entered the doors of my clinic, and I gave him a great big bear hug. What my staff did not know was that he was an old patient of mine whom I had not seen in three years.

After we laughed out loud with mutual joy, I said, "Man, I thought you were dead!"

He said from behind his long, scraggily beard, "No, Doc, I was just locked up for a minute."

My secretary started spraying air freshener behind us as I led my friend to my office. I was the only staff member who did not get overwhelmed by his odor or bitten by his bugs. All I could sense was that the man's love for God, kindled by our conversations three years ago, was still shining brightly after all these years. I would like to share with you a poem by E. P. He is one of my most spiritual patients, but he refers to himself only as a "wounded child of God."

The Precious Gift of Unconditional Love

I heard God's calling
He knows me by name,
Many times I walked away
And I am to blame.

He reached out His Almighty healing hand
And said, "You need not be afraid."
So I fell to my knees and started to pray.

He took me by my hands
And led me to a peaceful place,
Where the soothing winds
Caressed my face.

As He told me He was leaving
But only for a while,
God blessed me with a gift
With an ever loving smile.

He said, "My precious, precious child
Take heed to what I say,
You can only keep my gift
If you give it away."

—E. P. (Wounded Child of God)

CHAPTER 3

Meeting God's Purpose

W hy did I get involved in the treatment of HIV back in the late 1970s? To put it very simply, I was studying to be a doctor and people were dying. You had to be courageous to treat HIV in the late 1970s, because there was so little we knew about how it could be spread. In early 1991, I became Director of Clinics for the Rockland County Health Department. Having been trained in New York City, I knew this epidemic would soon spread into the suburbs of New York. In late 1991, Dr. Marvin Thalenberg, the commissioner of the health department, and I hatched a plan to start the first HIV clinic in Rockland County. By that time, the basketball player Magic Johnson had announced he had contracted HIV. HIV awareness had been born. In 2005, I opened an HIV clinic in the Bronx.

Dr. Thalenberg informed me that I would soon treat the patients at the new HIV clinic, and he gave me this advice: "If you love your patients, you will learn whatever it is that you need to know, and you will succeed." This advice, from my Jewish boss, was like the final advice Jesus gave to his disciples: "Love one another." The advice is as profound as it is simple. I did love my patients, but still it was a daunting task to be the only doctor to treat Rockland County's subpopulation consisting mostly of heroin addicts and prostitutes, for a disease in which the life expectancy from the time of diagnosis was less than two years. But I had to open the HIV clinic, largely because of the stories of my patients' broken lives. Here are some of their stories.

An HIV-infected heroin addict told me she wanted to have a baby, but she did not want to take HIV medication to reduce the risk of vertical transmission of HIV to the baby (from 33 percent to 8 percent). Her reasoning was that she deals with a fifty-fifty chance of dying each day, because of her addiction, so that a 33 percent chance of her baby getting HIV was not bad in comparison.

A thirteen-year-old girl came to the Sexually Transmitted Disease (STD) clinic where she presented us with no fewer than three diseases. We treated her and advised her to make an appointment with the Planned Parenthood clinic, to which she scoffed, "Planned Parenthood? I'm not planning to have a family!"

A patient once told me that he was a "calendar crack addict." I asked him to explain. He said he would only do crack on the first and fifteenth of every month, because that is when the welfare checks came. Another patient told me that it was a common strategy for a thirteen-year-old girl to come to this country, have multiple babies, and live on welfare and other government benefits (health care, food stamps, and housing). The law was changed by President Clinton's Welfare Reform Bill, which put an eighteen-month cap per child on welfare. Otherwise, we would encourage generations of welfare babies to be born. Entitlements from the government, if left unchecked, can decay our society and spread poverty. **(Bronxism: the Medicaid card is the poor man's credit card.)**

We can laugh now, because HIV is no longer the death sentence it was in the early 1980s. HIV is now a chronic disease. I tell my patients that they are more likely to die by walking into the street while talking on a cell phone, or from a bullet in a drive-by shooting.

There is definitely a lighter side to dealing with the underserved. Humor is the best medicine, and I have met some of the funniest people while treating HIV in the Bronx. Rich and poor people can have some common experiences. I pondered this as I fried my Thanksgiving turkey for the first time. I imagined myself on fire, running up and down the street, only to catch up with black comedian, Richard Pryor, who infamously caught on fire and ran up and down the street when his crack pipe exploded! Nobody has a monopoly on stupidity.

I have a toothless, elderly, black HIV patient, who is originally from the South, who came to my clinic with pneumonia. I wrote him prescriptions for antibiotics and cough syrup, and as he got up to leave my office, he stopped and asked, "Hey, Doc, you got any of *those pills?*"

Perplexed, I asked, "Do you mean Viagra?" I thought, *This will be death by libido* and said, "You cannot have sex! Sex will kill you in your weakened state!"

The man paused for a moment, then said, "Doc, when I was born, I came out of one, and when I die I want to be going back in." (His terminology had to be toned down, and it definitely loses something in the translation.) **(Bronxism: the number one cause of death in the Bronx is stupidity.)**

What if one of my patients was really an angel sent by God to test my intentions and my love for people? I often think of this when I see a grungy, smelly, angry crack addict who wants what he wants "right now." In most cases, feeding my patients pizza averts irritability, and my six-foot-four, three-hundred-fifty pound, former army ranger and now security guard handles the other cases. **(Bronxism: a person with a poor attitude becomes a magnet for unpleasant experiences.)** Jesus had a fish that fed five thousand, and I have a pizza that feeds fifty. Someone once called my clinic "Dr. Ibrahim's Clinic and Pizzeria. Take two slices and call me in the morning." Food tends to quiet people down, especially if they have not eaten in three days because they have been on a crack cocaine run. **(Bronxism: people will change when they see that the pain of staying the same outweighs the pain of changing.)** I have warned drunken patients that if they want to come to my clinic drunk, then they have to bring enough booze for me and all the staff. I tell the crack addicts that the only crack they should have is "the crack in your behind." **(Bronxism: addiction is like chasing a grizzly bear because you want a fur coat!)** On the contrary, you don't have to chase the best things in life, as they are free. The best things don't come with strings attached, and if you do right, the best things seem to chase you! Here is another poem by E. P. (Wounded Child of God):

21

The Only Friend Who Stayed

Walking through the darkness
Even though it was the light of day,
My addiction took me places
At a very high price to pay.

Blinded by a veil of confusion,
False evidence presented an illusion.

I was imprisoned and had a
Distorted reality,
I contemplated suicide as a
Way to flee my insanity.

Through the many friends that I've
Deceived and the bridges I've burned,
This is the greatest lesson
That I finally learned.

Deep within me lies a worthy heart,
A precious gem,
I won't give it away for just a
Hit off the crack stem.

Now I no longer wonder
And yet I do not understand,
Why Jesus never left me
And always held my hand.

—E. P. (Wounded Child of God)

22

But what if God plans to use one of my patients to accomplish His will? What if God put me in their path to feed them, show them His love, and give them medicine to keep them alive at least until they can know the love of Jesus? What if the thirteen-year-old girl at the STD clinic, or that thirteen-year-old immigrant girl who was birthing welfare babies, was to one day have a son or daughter who would become a great preacher, or a prophet? It would not be the first time God used a poor, plain, lowly person to accomplish His will. God enjoys using the foolish things of this world to confound the wise. The Bible speaks of an immigrant teenage girl who God used to change the world: her name was Mary and her son was Jesus.

God is concerned with our intention, our motivation, and our heart. God uses people who show spiritual fortitude by having faith and spreading love, even in times of great distress. *Great burden* brings out *greater love*. Mary and Joseph, the parents of Jesus, were very poor and were immigrants in a foreign land. God enjoys making something out of nothing. Jesus was not born in a hospital or even in a bed, but in an animal manger. From his humble beginning, Jesus would fulfill God's plan for all humanity. Other examples of humble beginnings: Muhammad was an orphan, and Moses's mother cast him into a river in a cradle of reeds. (See the essay in chapter 10, "The River of God's Mercy.")

What if I stood in the way of God's plan, and I let my personal bias stop me from showing love to my patients? How can I know what God's plan is for my patients and for me? The answer is through prayers. God invented prayer so we could have a conversation with Him; God loves to talk heart-to-heart with His creation. In Jeremiah 33:3, God advises the prophet Jeremiah, "Call to me and I will answer you and tell you great and unsearchable things that you do not know." God will provide us answers to questions that we did not even have the wisdom to ask, if only we cry out to Him, as did the prophet Jeremiah, and the mother of Moses when she was distraught over Pharaoh's decree to kill all Jewish sons.

When we pray, we ought to be far more concerned with what God will say to us, than with what we intend to tell Him. God already knows our needs. There is no value in petitioning God through flowery, repetitive, ritualistic prayers—these kind of prayers are like a laundry list to God; we come away empty from ritualistic prayers, because although we created a noise in God's ear, we never stopped babbling long enough to hear God speak to our souls. Fervent prayer is all about spending time with God, not our ability to tell Him what we need.

The fervent prayers of an Aborigine Indian can be just as honorable in God's eye as the fervent prayers of a modern-day scholar. "For the wisdom of this world is foolishness in God's sight" (1 Corinthians 3:19). The simple man has the same opportunity to offer fervent prayer as the intellectual man—the Christian, the Muslim, the Jew. We all have the same opportunity for God to honor our prayers, as long as these prayers are fervent and frequent. But how often are religious people guilty of just going through the motions of prayer without really crying out to God? God honors us when we cry out to Him and we listen for His answer, just as the prophet Jeremiah did, and King David when he prayed with a "broken and contrite heart" (Psalm 51:17).

CHAPTER 4

A Muslim Meets Jesus (In Visions and in Dreams)

It seems that many Muslims become closet Christians after having had a private encounter with Jesus in a dream or in a vision. It was God's plan to send us Jesus, but who is to say that a Muslim's private encounter with Jesus cannot bring salvation? I am out of the closet, but I would never judge another person's salvation just because I was unfamiliar with the manner that Jesus entered into that person's life. My own Christianity probably started some seven years before I proclaimed it, or even knew it in my mind. Who is to say that my earliest encounter with Jesus carried a less legitimate seal of salvation than if I had received Jesus through a team of splendid Christian evangelists? There is nothing sweeter than meeting Jesus as you are, where you are, and when you are alone. When Jesus comes to you, in a dream or in a vision, you become intimately acquainted with God's love. There is no greater friend then he who laid down his life for you as did Jesus. I want to open this chapter with the recollection of a dream I had about the sacrifice of Jesus: The Wooden Cross.

The Wooden Cross

I dreamed that Jesus Christ was going to be preaching at the Vatican and some of my Christian friends and I wanted to get a glimpse of him. In preparation for our trip, we all shaved our heads and put on simple white tunics. Being that I was a Muslim, I thought to myself, *We all look like a bunch of Muslims ready for the pilgrimage to Mecca.*

However, one important detail made us distinctly Christian: we each wore simple wooden crosses around our necks. The crosses were made of rough wood. They were jagged, full of splinters, and they draped over our necks with a white cotton string.

We all stood outside the Vatican, impressed by the size and the architecture of the cathedral. I felt a little embarrassed to be in such an awe-inspiring place with a baldpate, barefoot, and dressed in a simple white tunic.

When the doors of the sanctuary opened, we moved against a crowd of people who were trying to get out. The people were rushing, as if they were exiting a subway train at the Fifty–Ninth Street Station in Manhattan, New York City. A conductor's voice on the loudspeaker said, "Let 'em out first, watch the closing doors!" As we pushed our way inside, I noticed that the people leaving the sanctuary wore ornate gold chains around their necks, and on the chains hung diamond-studded, golden crucifixes.

Once inside, we again marveled at the architecture—high ceilings and gold everywhere! The people were dressed like soldiers of ancient Rome with gaudy golden helmets and golden armor, and they carried golden spears. I thought that this armor would be useless in real battle, because gold is such a soft metal.

Then I saw a man who looked like Jesus—chubby, smiling, with red cheeks. I could not tell if it was really Jesus, because he did not resemble the emaciated, suffering, rendition of Christ that I had seen in pictures. Twelve people, who resembled disciples, sat around this man. One turned to our small group and said, "We will show you humble ones what is true joy, so much joy that you will dance on a leaf while it is still on the tree!"

At this remark from the disciple, the man who looked like Jesus smiled at us and nodded in agreement, though he did not say a word. The next moment, the disciples began to sing the hymn, "Oh, Mighty Cross." The Roman soldiers would not sing, but the group from our church immediately joined in. Our voices cracked with emotion; our faces were covered with tears of adoration.

As we sang, I clutched the small wooden cross around my neck. Thankful that Jesus had loved me, I took delight when my hand was pierced by a little splinter from my cross. At the same moment my finger was pierced, I could feel the eyes of the man who resembled Jesus look at me. He was somehow attuned to every human suffering, even the minor suffering caused by my little wooden splinter. The words he said, "I too had a cross, and it too had splinters, but my cross also had nails," assured me that he was the living Christ.

Hearing this, we all knew we were in front of the real Jesus Christ, and we fell at his feet. A wonderful sense of peace covered us. We were all grateful that our crosses were not made of gold, but rather of rough wood, and we were all grateful that our crosses, although they had splinters, did not have nails.

On December 16, 1998, I gave my life to Jesus Christ. My wife will say that the time was long overdue; the Cuban brother who lovingly evangelized to me will say that it happened too fast (he had only known me a week); and my Muslim parents will say it should never have happened at all! These are the perceptions of mortals—in God's time, it was the right time to find the love of Jesus. Below is an essay I wrote that describes the events that led to my finding Christ.

The Right Time Is God's Time

My parents are Shiite Muslims from Pakistan who lived on the India side of the border when the violent partition of India and Pakistan took place in 1947. My father, a medical doctor, raised his family in India for a few years before moving back to Pakistan. I was born when my parents later visited India, and when I was three years old, we moved to America. When I was twelve, my parents joined an American Sufi *tarika* (group), and they became very active in a small Sufi mosque, which they attend to this day. My family members are the only born Muslims in this Sufi *tarika*; everyone else was an American convert to Islam. For many years, I considered myself a devout Sufi Muslim, always seeking to know Allah through *Erfan* (the way to knowing God), but despite the observance of prayers, fasting, and other Islamic duties, I fell short of achieving my goal to know God. My unfulfilled quest to know Allah left me in a state of despair, yet I clung to an old Sufi saying, "You, who thirst for the tea, do not realize that the tea also thirsts for you."

One day as a young man working in my carpentry shop, I realized that this Sufi adage was true. I was building some furniture when suddenly I heard a voice very clearly say, "Jesus too was a carpenter." I looked around and shouted, "Who said that?" But I was alone in my carpentry shop!

I even asked my wife if Jesus had been a carpenter. "Why do you want to know?"

I answered, "No reason."

Two years later, still a Muslim, I remember watching TV when a two-minute blurb came on about the Promise Keepers march in Washington DC. Two million Christian men marched to profess their faith and their commitment to serve God and their families. Tears came to my eyes as I watched men of every race and color hug one another, and I saw some of them praying in small, circular groups. My heart wanted to join them, but my head reminded me that I was a Muslim and I did not belong. Two more years had to pass before I became a Christian, but in retrospect, I now realize that through these events, God was drawing me to Him. The tea was thirsty for me.

Thus began a process that imperceptibly led me to follow Jesus Christ. I did not even know that while I was seeking God, God was seeking me. Why me? I am so imperfect, so small. Sure, I fought changing my religion, but it was God's master plan. Was I the right person for God to enter into? Was it the right time? Was it the right way?

The power of God was waiting to lift me, but too often, I was unaware of His presence. God allowed trouble into my life in order to get my attention, and with my back against a wall, trouble made me cry out to God. My life was in shambles one month before I became a Christian. My marriage was on the rocks, I had been swindled out of a large sum of money, and worst of all, and my Sufi Muslim spiritual leader had just died. God permitted the water of life to come to boil and prepare me for the tea leaves of His Holy Spirit.

Something that helped me relate to Christians was my Sufi Muslim leader who would attend Christian churches when he was in Europe, far away from any mosques. He would explain to his perplexed entourage that he loved to pray alongside Christians, because he could feel the passion with which they praised the Lord. Still a Muslim, I came to enjoy praising God alongside Christians, just as my Sufi leader did. I didn't have a very good singing voice, and I didn't even know all the words to the beautiful worship songs. I just quietly moved my lips, usually with tears in my eyes. Nobody but my Lord knew that I cried during worship. Nobody but my Lord could hear me sing. My Lord hears me, and He loves the way I sing. He hears the words of my heart.

Considering myself a trespasser in any Christian church, I picked a church that displayed a sign that read **Trespassers are Welcome.** Once inside, I found the Christians joyful, friendly, and God-fearing, but I had a huge problem with their method of worship. I thought it was *irreverent* to have a five-piece band performing during worship! Was this a discotheque, or was this a place of worship? Before I became a Christian, I could not fully allow myself to *feel joy during worship.* I was like a man sitting in a *dark, silent room* for many years. The first few times I went to church, it was as if I had been thrown into a *noisy, sunny place.* I was blinded and deafened by the sights and sounds of Christians at worship. But God has a sense of humor. In a few years, he exalted my praises, and I sang baritone in a six-member worship team, like a Pakistani Barry White. The worship team included my second son, Russell, as the drummer.

When my Sufi leader passed away, I felt deeply saddened to the point of developing chest pains. Somehow, in the midst of my troubles, I got on my knees and cried out to Allah, "Oh, Allah, I know that you love me! I know that you have something better for your servant! Show me a sign and whatever it is, I will obey!" (**Bronxism: God knows that we respond to Him not because we see the light, but more often because we feel the heat.**)

Trouble is God's little wake-up call. Our vision becomes clear when our backs are up against a wall. Two weeks later, my wife approached me with an invitation to a forgiveness seminar at a Christian church. This seminar was the sign I had been waiting for, and little did I know that the seminar would not only start a healing process in my marriage, but I would also meet a certain Cuban man who would bring me to Jesus Christ. We must come to God as King David did in Psalm 51. King David had a "broken and contrite heart," and God needed to bring in the bulldozer to clear out my old life and take me to my knees before He could lay the foundation for my new life. I am reminded of Jeremiah 33:3, where God instructs the prophet, "Cry out to me, and I will answer you and tell you great and unsearchable things you do not know." God answered my prayers with such totality that He gave me answers to questions I didn't even ask. **(Bronxism: keep PUSHing. PUSH stands for "pray until something happens.")**

Twenty-five years ago, I met my wife, a Christian, while I was completing my residency program. I persuaded her to marry me and to become a Muslim. She remained a Muslim for ten years, but then she returned to Christianity during a tumultuous period in our marriage. I did not want to interfere with her Christian faith, because I could see that it brought her solace at a difficult time in our lives. Furthermore, I knew if that I forced her to choose between her faith and me, I would clearly be the loser. I permitted my wife to attend church, but I faithfully took our children to our Islamic Sunday school where my father taught. I permitted my wife to sometimes take the children to church with her, partly because I wasn't sure of my own religious identity, and partly because I didn't want my children to miss out on Christian teachings.

One Sunday, I was at home watching football on television. My six-year-old daughter came to me and smilingly professed she had gone to her mother's church, and that she is now a Christian. I went ballistic! First, I scolded my daughter and told her that she was still a Muslim. Because of my scolding, she started weeping uncontrollably. Next, I cornered my wife and demanded to know what sort of trick she was playing, changing our daughter's religion behind my back!

My wife said, "If your child comes to you hungry, you must give her food. So when our daughter came up to me with spiritual hunger, I couldn't deny her nourishment!" My wife then calmly explained that this was no trick, but rather an act of God. It seems, on that very morning, my mother had called my wife from the Islamic Sunday school and said that our daughter had an upset stomach.

When my wife went to pick her up, my daughter got into the car and pleaded, "I want to go to church with you, Mommy!"

My wife asked, "What about the stomach ache?"

"It's gone, Mommy!"

My wife told me that she had been praying for a sign from God to let her know how to raise the children, as Muslims or as Christians. Our daughter's zeal for going to church was the sign my wife was waiting for. At church, my daughter ran up to the altar like an arrow when the pastor asked for those who wanted to accept Jesus Christ as their personal savior. On the way home, my daughter told her mother, "Today is the happiest day of my life, now that I am a Christian!"

After I heard my wife's explanation, I calmed down a bit. Then my daughter approached me with tears in her eyes and asked, "Daddy, if I have to be a Muslim, can I at least read my Bible?" I started to feel bad for having scolded her on her happy day.

"Of course, you can," I said.

My daughter continued, "And Daddy, today they celebrated Father's Day at church. All the daddies got up and went to the altar, but you weren't there."

I thought to myself, *Of course not, I was home watching football.*

My daughter went on, "Promise me, Daddy, that on the next Father's Day you will go to church. Please, for me."

My heart began to melt and I told my daughter, "Of course, I'll be there for you!"

Then she smiled, reached up, and hugged my legs.

Six months before the following Father's Day, I started to attend church with my family.

The pastor at the new church was very kind to me. He invited me to discuss religion with him. Through all my questions for the pastor, God was bringing me to a boil so that soon I would be ready for His tea leaves. I could see that the pastor had a genuine concern for me, even though I couldn't always understand his answers. I began to meet the pastor once a week for about eight weeks. I tried to convince him that I was merely a Muslim who loved Christians, an observer from the outside looking in. He patiently listened to my problems with religious identity, and he shared his thoughts with me as well as read verses from the Bible. I asked the pastor many questions. Chapter 8 will offer answers to these commonly asked questions by Muslims: What is the concept of the Holy Trinity? Why do Christians call Jesus the Son of God? How could Jesus's death on the cross serve as an atoning sacrifice for our sins? How can the sacrifice of one man usher in the salvation of so many? Why would God send Jesus, a baby, to do a man's job?

Once, I angrily accused the pastor and all Christians for being arrogant, because they insisted that the only way to know God is through Jesus Christ. I remember taunting the pastor with the following question: "If a serial killer knows Jesus, does he go to heaven, while my dear old Muslim mother, who does not know Jesus, goes to hell?"

I would not be a Christian today if my pastor answered that question in any way other than the way he did. My pastor said, "Only God judges. It is not for me or any other man to judge the sincerity of a serial killer's plea for salvation, even if this plea is spoken one week or one minute before his death by execution. As for your mother, we do not know if Jesus has come to her in a dream, or in some vision. In some hidden way, Jesus might have made himself known to her. God is merciful; He honors those who fervently seek Him. God would not put someone in hell who has never heard the Gospel of Jesus Christ, but has cried out to Him as a seeker; however, as for you (my pastor was talking to me in his office), it is too late for you to turn your back on Jesus Christ. You have already heard the Gospel, and you will suffer grave consequences if you denounce the name of Jesus, because Jesus was God's plan for your salvation."

As a Muslim, I wondered why God would send Jesus, as a baby, to do a man's job. God did not want to conquer us; instead, He sent someone so irresistible that we could not help but love him. God was making an understatement when He sent a baby to live and love with us. God was teaching us that love is a subtle process. In my last days as a Muslim,

I found that Christianity became irresistible to me, not because of its dogma, but because of the love and kindness of Christians. What made Christianity irresistible to me? In a single word—love! The love of my six-year-old daughter. The love and kindness of Christ reflected in the face of my Christian daughter, who also came to me as a baby.

Through all the Christian people around me, God was bombarding me with love. God used a loving Cuban man, Manny, to lead me to Christ. This man never hit me over the head with theological arguments or biblical scriptures; instead, he was kind in his dealing with me. That kindness was Christ's love in him, and Christ's love compelled me to respond. I had met my Cuban brother only a week earlier at the forgiveness seminar. He came to my house to watch a football game with me. (See how God can turn around the significance of a football game?) My Cuban brother had the Bible in one hand and microwavable popcorn in the other. First, we put the television on mute during the commercials and we talked about God, and then we put it on mute during the game. Finally, we turned the television off altogether, because the conversation became too intense for any distraction. My Cuban brother focused on what our two religions had in common, and how, in a society that devalues God, we have but one common enemy—Satan. We talked until two in the morning, never growing tired, never caring that we each had to wake up early to go to work.

The most memorable thing my Cuban brother said was, "You're a Muslim, and our wives are Christians. I am a Christian, but we should all pray together. You can pray on your prayer rug, we will pray the way we are accustomed to, but we should pray together!"

Those simple words broke my heart, and I knew that I would be a fool to turn my back on this love and understanding shown to me by my Cuban brother. My brother had no self-serving motives, and he wasn't feeding his ego. He just wanted what was right for me. Later that same morning, I telephoned him and told him I was ready to come to Christ. He said the angels were rejoicing! Throughout the years, Manny and I have remained the closest of friends, and our wives say that Manny and I talk to each other on the phone like a couple of teenage girls. I think they are just jealous!

The next day, I had a dream that confirmed my decision to become a Christian. I dreamed I was in a hospital conference room where doctors met to discuss cases. On the table were about ten thousand charts. The charts were from every patient I had ever seen. Standing next to me, in his white robe and looking at me with penetrating eyes, was none other than Jesus Christ—the master physician. He motioned to me with his hands and said, "Bring them to me and I will heal them." In my dream, I wept profusely as I drew up one chart after the other, laboriously finding each patient's phone number, calling them, and telling them to come to Jesus.

When I awoke, I ran to the church to tell the pastor of my dream. On that day, I boldly told the pastor, "I don't want your Christianity, just give me Christ so that I can know God! I don't need to learn a completely new belief system with a new set of pointless rituals and customs, because as a Muslim, I already have too many rituals and customs. Just give me Christ!"

My pastor recognized what the Lord was saying to me through that dream, and he immediately gave me an assignment. He told me about an extremely depressed man at the mental hospital where I worked. I was to seek him out, lay my hands on him, and pray for his depression to lift. I found the patient and told him two things. I told him that I had just become a Christian, and that last night I had a dream in which Christ told me to bring my patients to Him so that He could heal them. Suddenly coming out of his withdrawn mood, he asked, "Are you going to lay hands on me?"

I answered "Yes." Then I reluctantly placed my hands on his shoulders. (I didn't know the first thing about laying hands on someone!) We both closed our eyes. There was a long pause. "Aren't you going to pray for me?" he asked.

"Go easy on me man, I've only been a Christian for thirty-five hours!"

Then a miraculous thing happened. God's grace (known by Christians as the Holy Spirit) took over. This severely depressed, almost catatonic, man said, "Keep your hands on my shoulders, and I'll pray for myself." Then he proceeded to belt out a beautiful healing prayer—everything from headaches to hangnails. I was amazed. Only minutes ago, this man could hardly even speak! Two days later, the man was discharged from the mental ward. Although he's been back a few times, I know that he's equipped with faith, hope, and Christ's healing love. Praying aloud with someone is the greatest expression of empathy. For a few moments, you put down your agenda and take the time and interest to feel somebody's pain. Praying with my patients greatly enhances the doctor-patient relationship, because it honors a higher relationship—the relationship we each have with God.

That afternoon, I saw one of my crack-addicted AIDS patients. I love ministering to crack addicts. I tell them how lucky they are to be crack addicts; they're lucky because Christ always comes looking for His one lost sheep. I tell them, "Christ loves all ninety-nine of his sheep, but He especially loves the sinner who knows that he is lost. You could be that one lost sheep!"

This crack-addicted AIDS patient came to me from jail. He wore heavy chains. I told him, "Just because you're in chains and I'm a doctor, don't think God loves me more than He loves you. In God's eyes, we are the same. Just until this morning, I was also in chains until the Lord lifted me!"

The man and I wept. We prayed. A few months later, he was out of jail, the seed had been planted, and his girlfriend had been praying. He came to my church and accepted Christ. He remained crack-free, eventually attended a Christian retreat for substance abusers, and his AIDS is under control even without medication. All praise is to God.

In America, there is a movement to keep prayer out of our schools, government, and the workplace. My supervisors told me not to pray with my patients, and I was advised not to share biblical scriptures with them. One of the reasons I left my Rockland County job as the director of clinics in favor of private practice was because God is my only boss.

On December 16, 1998, I gave my life to Jesus Christ, and since then, I openly pray with my patients. As a Muslim doctor, while at home on my prayer mat, I would secretly pray for my patients but would not tell them. Now I pray openly, aloud, and in the company of my patients. Prayer definitely belongs in the medical profession, because Jesus Christ is the master physician. As a doctor, I treat patients, but only God cures. I would be happy to be a hangnail on a pinkie finger on the healing hand of God.

I never argue about religion in order to poison someone's mind about their faith, or to bring about their conversion. I do not like the word "conversion"; I prefer "transformation." We are transformed by God's love. As a Muslim, I used to tell evangelizing Christians, "To you, your religion, to me, mine."

As a Christian, I find it hard to make that statement, because it is too neutral. As a Christian, I have a passion to share my heart, my testimony, and my newly found love for Jesus Christ. A change in heart only comes by God's grace, not man's tongue. We do not come to know God through anyone's convincing or through mental gymnastics. "For the wisdom of this world is foolishness in God's sight" (1 Corinthians 3:19). The only purpose of intellect is so that we can share with others what we have learned through our hearts. By God's grace alone, our heart changes, then our nature changes, and lastly, after repetition of the new behavior, our mind is changed. In Luke 10:27, it is said, "Love thy Lord with all thy heart, soul (i.e., nature), strength (i.e., behavior), and mind." It is fascinating that this scripture describes the same transformative progression by which I came to know God.

I came home from work that December day glowing with spirituality! Wanting to see if my wife would notice a change in me, I waited a week before I told her that I had become a Christian. When I finally told her, she was overjoyed but not surprised. Then I came to know something interesting. Three weeks prior to my conversion, she would put her hand on me and pray for me at night while I was sleeping. Other nights, the Lord would wake her up at three o'clock in the morning, she would go downstairs, get on her knees, and cry out to God for her husband to understand the love of Christ. God began to work in my life in answer to her prayers. My wife and I eventually renewed our wedding vows in a Christian ceremony. This was to honor both of our individual relationships with the Lord, so that the Lord would honor our relationship with each other. Our three children made three wedding cakes for the event. Good things have started to happen in our marriage that neither of us could have foreseen.

CHAPTER 5

Male Meets Female (The Shell Meets the Yolk)

When I first set eyes on the woman who later became my wife, I shouted, "Allah has favored me!" Twenty-five years, three children, two dogs, and one religion later, I look at the same woman and say, "The Lord is trying to whip me into shape!"

My wife, Anne, tells me that as a girl she always prayed that God would give her a spiritual husband. She told me that God had spoken to her when we first met, and that God told her that I would be her husband. But of course, back in the disco era, many a young woman had a similar epiphany when I used my baritone ventriloquism. I would come strutting by, sporting a mustache, elevator shoes, my long hair, my baritone voice, and gold chains. She was beautiful, but I was more beautiful. (**Bronxism: beauty is what beauty does. A fat, homely girl who cooks for you is better than a sleek, sexy one who cheats behind your back and leaves you.**) Besides, in the words of Abbott and Costello, if the fat homely girl leaves, who cares? She was fat and homely to begin with.

When my Anne found out that I was a Muslim, she got angry with God for not giving her a Christian man. She asked me if she was going to be the first of my many wives. I told her that one wife was like a single hole in the head, and that if I had a second wife, my brains would leak out twice as fast; therefore, I intended to be monogamous.

"And what about your seventy-two virgins waiting for you in heaven?" she asked while I was watching baseball.

"In heaven, the wives do not take the TV remote from their husbands, and besides, I do not want seventy-two holes in my head." That explanation was enough for her. Thankfully, she had set her standards very low. She and I were married three months after we met, but for fourteen years, she wondered why God never gave her a Christian man. It was apparently God's fault she had fallen in love with a Muslim instead of a Christian. **(Bronxism: when it comes to staying with your spouse, "The devil you know is better than the devil you don't know," and "Don't be too quick to give up on the alcoholic, only to find your next spouse is a heroin addict.")**

I had a very rudimentary concept of marriage. My belief went something like this: a husband should be kind to his wife, and although he should not be deaf to his wife's intuitive heartfelt advice, his wife must obey her husband as long as he is bringing her toward the light of God. An Islamic proverb describes a Godly wife to be like her husband's shadow. If her husband turns his back on the light of God, the shadow grows large and runs away. If her husband walks toward the light, the shadow shrinks and finds its place behind him. Feminists would not take too kindly to that proverb, but they would probably jump out of their skin upon hearing the following quote from the Koran, which gives men the right to have sex anytime with their wives. Sura 2 (Al Baqarah), verse 223: "Your wives are as tilth soil unto you; so approach your tilth when or how you will."

In the above passage from the Koran, wives are called "tilth soil," or "dirt." But I have never seen a Muslim woman treated as dirt in my thirty-eight years as an American Muslim. I am proud to be an American. My parents brought me to America when I was only three years old, so my understanding of how Muslim men treat their women is largely based on my parents' example of Islamic family life. My parents have been married for almost sixty years, and my father has always cared for my mother with the utmost kindness and respect. I am not in a position to judge how Muslim women are treated in the Middle East, based on my limited experience traveling outside the United States. It is quite possible that women's rights are trampled by Middle Eastern men, but women are mistreated elsewhere in the world, just more insidiously so, even by non-Muslim men. In America, men are responsible for a disproportionately large amount of rape and other violent crimes, as compared to American women; no doubt testosterone is to blame, not only for a man's libido, but also for his aggression, irrespective of his religious beliefs or nationality.

Quite often, the American husband's response to not getting enough sex with his wife is to have an affair, or go gay, or both. Personally, I have not known any Muslim man with more than one wife; this is because it is nearly impossible to "Love all your wives equally," as commanded by the Koran. I have heard of polygamous Arab sheiks with their blonde-haired, blue-eyed, gold-digger American wives, yet everyone involved has consented to the polygamous arrangement. At least, if a Muslim man has multiple wives, he will be faithful to them, and he must show them all equal love and financial support—contrast this to an American deadbeat dad who has multiple mistresses. The deadbeat dad will be late with his child support payments for the children that he is aware of, and will pay nothing for the children he claims are not his. He will not pay until he is forced to get a paternity test and a cameo appearance on the *Jerry Springer Show*.

In Islam, women wear modest clothing to help limit sexual temptation. In Western nations, some women prance about half-naked for the sole purpose of selling something in an advertisement. The divorce rate in Western countries is more than 50 percent compared to 1 or 2 percent in Muslim countries, and no, that is not because Muslim men hit their wives harder than American men.

What about motherhood? The Koran states, "Heaven is at the feet of mothers." How is motherhood looked upon in the West? America is one of the richest countries in the world, yet it has an embarrassingly high infant mortality rate, worse than many Third World nations. Women's health issues are put on the back burner far too often. For example, the recommended age of a woman's first mammogram was raised from forty to fifty. I feel it should be lowered to thirty-five. One in eleven American women will get breast cancer. Earlier screening saves lives, but the policy makers tell us it costs too much to screen younger women. Why should our society only be a "man's world"? Although women's rights are lacking in the Middle East, America also has a lot of work to do when it comes to the rights of women, children, and unborn children. Abortion goes against the principles of Islam and Christianity.

I had a lot to learn about women. Miraculously, the very first two times I randomly opened a Bible, God led me to read the following two scriptures: the first one reminded me that women are the "weaker partner" (1 Peter 3:7), but the second scripture said that God's power "is made perfect in weakness" (2 Corinthians 12:9–10). **(Bronxism: women may seem weak, but they are attached to a powerful God.)**

Women are generally more receptive to God and more perceptive of His signs as compared to men. The praying wife gives meaning to her husband's life. In an Islamic proverb, the yolk of an egg gives meaning to the shell. God has partnered the shell to the yolk for the yolk's protection and to prevent wastage of the yolk's life-giving gift. Sometimes my wife is the keeper of my covenant to God. On the other hand, I am sometimes the keeper of her earthly life. I have noticed that in the best marriages, those that have lasted fifty years or more, the husband and wife drink from each other's cup—she from his worldly cup, he from her spiritual cup. I know that my wife is a ray of God's light shining for me to fulfill the goals God has set for me and for our children, and for this, she was definitely worth giving up Sunday afternoon football. **(Bronxism: a good cooking woman keeps a family together. Either your kids will be breaking bread with their families, or they'll be pulling triggers with their "homies.")**

The un-manliest thing a husband can do is to argue toe-to-toe with his wife. Do not enter the boxing ring with her. Give her an excuse not to fight. Tell her that your boxing gloves are missing the laces, tell her that your boxing robe is in the wash, and tell her that your boxing grandmother is visiting from out of town. Do not accept her invitation to get in the ring with her! **(Bronxism: I have a mentally challenged patient who had the bad habit of getting phone numbers from women he would meet at mental institutions. I told him to stop picking up girls that way, because it is dangerous. But he replied, "Doc, those mental girls are really easy to pick up." Two months passed before the same guy** returned to my clinic, and this time he had scars all over his body from acid burns and ice-pick wounds. I asked, "What happened to you?" His answer was classic: "Doc, those mental girls are *easy to pick up,* but they're really *hard to put down!*")

A man who catfights with his wife is already the loser. He would be better off just taking his lumps from his wife and carving out a tiny bit of sanity in his "man cave." **(Bronxism: the barbershop epiphany. While getting my hair cut, the man in the chair to my left asked me, "How can you tell how long a man has been married?" "I don't know," I replied. He continued, "It's like the rings on a tree, only you have to count the lumps on his head, one for every year of marriage!" I thought that was rather clever, so I turned to the old man on my right to see if he was laughing. I was shocked to see that the old man had a perfectly formed, cone-shaped, bald head. I immediately lowered my eyes in embarrassment. Knowing what I must be thinking, he quipped, "Yeah, and my head is what happens when you're married forty-five years, and all the little lumps come together!" I thought to myself, *Monogamy is good—at least he doesn't have forty-five holes in his head*.)**

A man can either be right or he can be wrong, but *a woman has a third option*—she can be *adorable*. A man cannot be adorable. I would never tolerate a male friend if he behaved in a random and emotional, yet adorable, manner; he would quickly and permanently lose me as his friend. Without sounding too patronizing, a good man will find things about his wife that endear her to him. It could be how she wrinkles her nose when she laughs, or her poor sense of direction, or how she predictably forgets where she put something, or how she gets prettier when she is angry. (Okay, now I am patronizing.) Instead of a man demanding that his wife owns up to her mistakes, or judges her as he would another man, the good man says, *"Vive la différence!"*

I learned the concept of female adorability from an old Greek waiter at our favorite restaurant. This waiter was happily married for more than fifty years to the same woman. He took out his pen and pad and asked my wife what she wanted to order. My wife was preoccupied texting someone while she gave her order. Next, I gave my order. The waiter was about to go back to the kitchen when my wife stopped him and gave him a different order. He politely asked, "Is that *in addition* to what you have already ordered, or is that *instead* of your other order?"

She looked adamantly at him and said, "I never ordered anything!"

For a moment, he quizzically looked at her and then at his pad, which he showed her, and said, "But I didn't order this myself."

My wife was beginning to get frustrated with him, though she wasn't going to admit that she had made two consecutive orders. He quickly backed down. "Yes, my beautiful lady, so what will you order?"

I sat there amazed at how the waiter subjugated himself. I later caught him in the hall on the way to the bathroom and said, "I'm sorry for that confusion."

He wisely and succinctly answered, "No problem. That's what makes them adorable!"

Real love takes on the other person's burden (1 Corinthians, chapter 13); sometimes *having great burden brings out greater love.* (**Bronxism: the Bronx love is the best love.**) A homeless couple shared this Bronxism with me. This couple would sleep on park benches during the warm months and huddle together in a hallway of a tenement building during the winter. They stayed together for survival, and they shared each other's burdens because they did not have the luxury of prolonged, petty infighting.

With another Bronx couple, the woman stabbed her husband in the shoulder during an alcoholic rage. Rather than getting his wound cared for in the hospital, the man stitched his wound himself with an unsterilized needle and thread and without anesthesia. Why did he not go to the hospital? He did not want his wife arrested for assault.

I asked yet another one of my "Bronx love" patients how his marriage was going, to which he answered, "Oh, she threw an iron at me, and she threw a knife at me, but other than that, we're doing just fine." Now that is what I call heroic, immovable, real love, which is the opposite of insanity love.

Insanity Love

Real love is measured by only one thing—how much time is someone willing to spend by your side. Even if this time is spent in silence, real love can be expressed through a look or a touch. Real love cannot be rushed, it takes time, and it cannot be expressed at a distance.

Insanity love is harmful to whomever it is directed; this blatantly superficial love, issued just to smooth over an inconvenient situation, can drive a person insane.

Insanity love will send you Hallmark cards, it will buy you expensive gifts, it will blow you kisses from afar, and it will give you insincere flattery. This love is not made to last, it is designed to serve the ulterior motives of the one who gives it.

Insanity love is like a cut flower that looks pretty in a vase until the water dries up. Real love knows that love never runs dry, because it is attached to the sea of God's love, which is endless!

Insanity love happens when you tell a girl you love her, but in return, she rejects you by telling you that you are "a really good friend."

Insanity love happens when a deadbeat father showers his child with expensive gifts, but never spends time with him.

Insanity love happens when a cheating husband buys his wife a diamond after she finds out about his affair.

Insanity love happens when parents tell their children how much they love them, but leave them with a nanny while they go on an adult vacation.

Insanity love happens when the elderly are forgotten in a nursing home, but are remembered at the reading of the will.

How can we stop this insanity? We cure it with a dose of real love. We can take the time to love someone slowly with a loving look and a loving touch.

Real love is when we choose to be there for our loved ones, no matter how long it takes or whatever the consequences to showing love.

Real love doesn't mind being wounded if it is for the good of its lover.

Real love exposes the lover's own vulnerability, as it bravely lowers its sword and shield so that it may catch its wounded lover before she falls.

Real love is what Jesus did for us on the cross. What if, instead of dying for our sins, Jesus took a more convenient, safer way to show his love for us? What if he blew us eternal kisses, or sent us Hallmark cards to hell? No, Jesus showed us perfect love by laying down his very life for his loved ones. Why can't we strive to love like Jesus? 1 John 4:16 says, "And so we know and rely on the love God has for us. God is love. Whoever lives in love, lives in God, and God in them."

Perfect love casts away fear and sets you free; insanity love creates anxiety, causes division, and seeks to control, possess, and imprison the one it pretends to love. 1 John 4:18 says, "There is no fear in love. But perfect love drives out fear, because fear has to do with punishment. The one who fears is not made perfect in love."

In retrospect, it is easy to see how my marriage almost ended in divorce fifteen years ago, before I knew the love of Jesus. Guilty of insanity love, this is how I used to be:

- I had no inner peace or joy; therefore, I became controlling, overbearing, and dominating.
- I was always giving glory to myself, as though my achievements were my own doing.
- I never listened to my wife's suggestions, and I often treated her like a doormat.
- I had a hard time taking no for an answer, and I would yell and scream at my wife when I thought she was disobedient.
- I was insensitive, self-centered, stubborn, proud, and arrogant.
- I was agitated and tense. I was impatient and disrespectful. When I had a bad day at work, I handled stress by taking it out on my wife and children.
- I was blind to the love my wife had for me; thus, I became insecure and jealous.

As a fifty-year-old man, I can now boldly claim that I understand women, because I have *first learned how to understand myself.* This is how I would describe myself now, after having found the love of Jesus:

- I have a sense of peace and dignity that does not depend on how my wife treats me.
- I have acquired some of Christ's attributes, his thoughts, his attitude, his principles, and his heart; all of these have made me a better husband and father.
- I now consider my wife's opinion to be a valuable insight into my spiritual and secular life.
- I have learned it is better to serve my family than it is to be served by my family.
- I cheerfully turn to God on good and bad days, and never vent my frustrations on my family.
- I can now fully appreciate the love my wife has for me, because I see it as a reflection of the love that I have for Jesus Christ. Prayer and worship have become a regular part of my life.
- I have learned humility.
- I have a quiet confidence. I no longer have to justify my own worth—Jesus thought I was worth dying for and my dignity is with him.
- I have Christ's boldness, which enables me to deal wisely with my opponents and gain the respect of my friends.
- I am no longer a slave, but rather, I am a soldier.
- When I am victorious, I give glory to God, not myself.
- As I have been blessed by God, I have a passion to pass the blessing on to others.

CHAPTER 6

Body Odor Meets Perfume in a Subcompact Smart Car (My Spoof of *Men Are from Mars, Women Are from Venus*)

Why do some men drown their sorrows in alcohol? Could it be from the harsh reality that we men can never completely please our women? Or are men just escapists? Why do men delight in our bodily odors, while women hide these behind expensive perfumes? An unmarried man will eat cabbage and then ask you to pull his finger; an unmarried woman will retreat to the bathroom before passing gas. Until his wedding day, a man expects that little doves take his girl's feces to heaven: after the honeymoon, a new-smelling reality sets in.

Being of Pakistani descent, I feel it is my birthright to expertly discuss the subject of body odor. How can we help New York City cab drivers (many of them are my countrymen) get over their hydrophobia? Nevermind showering just for cleanliness—they will not shower to be clean. Perhaps they will take to soap and water, like a fish or a duck, when they learn to seek the refreshing quality of a morning shower. Or not. You cannot bait and switch Pakistanis; they are far too crafty. The French can also go a week or more without showering. I think that is why they invented perfume. The French are really Pakistanis in disguise—you can tell by their shared sense of hydrophobia.

Hydrophobia aside, why else would someone put on perfume? In the animal kingdom, smells are an important calling card. Animals mark their territories with urine, and they make sexy talk with pheromones. My dog, Seth, sneezes around people with strong perfumes, as if to say, "Why the mask? What are you trying to hide?" There is a lot I have learned from my dog, but I could never in a million years emulate my dog's incredible feats of love and loyalty (see chapter 11). My dog has taught me that people with dishonest smells are often guilty of other cover-ups that are sometimes called fashion. As for me, I like to be known as New York's worst-dressed doctor. I choose to dress this way, because I do not want to dress any better than the poorest patient I treat. Gandhi refused to wear anything but a loincloth because he also wanted to display solidarity with the poor.

I remember meeting my wife in a shopping mall having come straight from a bass fishing excursion at a local lake. I was dressed in my fishing vest, shorts, fishing hat—fully equipped with hanging lures, unmatched tube socks that were pulled up to my knees, and of course, sandals (Pakistanis like to wear socks and sandals). Not only did I scare the fish with my outfit, but I also scared my wife. She would not hold my hand or even walk within ten paces of me. Unfortunately, I constantly embarrass my wife with my poor fashion sense and my obesity; it seems the only time she is not embarrassed by me is when she goes to the bank. I may not have been fashionable at the mall, but at least there was no falsehood, and besides, that will be the last time she tells me to cut short my fishing trip so we can stroll the mall together.

At the mall I was ambushed by one of those perfume-spraying women while passing through Macy's with my wife. I stopped the lady and said, "Hold on, sister! I only have two smells: *bad* and *worse*. Don't try to give me a third one!" I do not try to hide my odors; it would be dishonest, and my dog would disapprove. My body odor shouts out to the animal kingdom, it harmonizes with a babbling brook, it whispers to the swaying pines, and this is what my body says: "Hey, somebody, get me some soap and water—I stink!"

What is the Smart Car all about? Is the car nothing more than a coffin with wheels, just waiting to be dispatched by an SUV? Or is it a gladiator pit where *body odor* can grapple with *perfume*? The man's "take me as I am" body odor collides with the woman's "guilt of odor" in the suffocating confines of a Smart Car—that sounds a lot like marriage. There isn't even any room for my dog, Seth. Seth is the wisest creature of olfaction among us; only he can translate the language of smell. Seth can't fit in the Smart Car. We are doomed if one of us passes gas and it creates a third smell. We can't even blame it on the dog.

Speaking of gas, what if the Smart Car runs out of fuel? Women have an *emotional gas tank,* which we good men must keep filled—or we risk having to push the car of our marriage to the next gas station, and it's entirely our fault. Oh, one more thing, *the fuel gauge is broken,* so good luck trying to figure out when she's empty! Again, you might wind up pushing the car. The good man keeps his wife's emotional tank topped off, always anticipating her needs and demonstrating his love for her through his actions. Sometimes *the emotional gas tank has a leak*—it is time to see a mechanic.

If *emotionality* is the major character flaw of women, then *escapism* is the major character flaw of men. We men with our macho odors get to be "badasses" when we are young, only to be whipped into shape by marriage. Meanwhile, women hiding behind their many secrets and prissy perfumes will eventually be eclipsed by age, gravity, and reality. Women need to learn how to *play fair* once marriage sets in. What happens when it all goes wrong and someone passes gas in the Smart Car, and there are too many conflicting smells and there is no dog? We get insanity love—and sometimes divorce.

It is written that "the truth shall set you free," but if it is spoken by a man, the truth shall make him lonely. *Never solve her problems,* even if she asks, because she would rather have you graciously revel in the emotionality of her predicament than offer a solution. She probably already knows the best solution, but she just wants to see how you squirm when she threatens to take some other capricious, costly way out. This is how she proves to herself that you love her more than you love your own rationality. As you show her your affection, the holes start to appear in your head, and your brains begin to leak out. Do not be concerned; you did not really need all those IQ points. If you *learn to gossip,* she will love you even more.

(Bronxism: sometimes it's more important to be happy than it is to be right.) Nevertheless, a husband must be exceedingly kind to his wife; he must anticipate her needs, protect her, and provide for her; and he must never intentionally hurt her. A husband must love his wife the way Christ loved the church—and Christ died for the church.

I never persist in fighting with my wife, because it is my mistake for disrupting her peace. **(Bronxism: if Mama ain't happy, nobody's happy.)** This is the secret to a long marriage: it is better to have many little fights than fewer, bigger ones. Consider this analogy: it is better to have a little cold and a little cough, because with the immune system activated, it is easier to avoid the flu. Here is an exercise for learning the futility of fighting: fight about many things that do not even matter, *so that you won't care if you lose*—and you might even have the opportunity to *admit you are wrong* and then *bow out of the argument gracefully*. You should fight every day *as if you don't mean it*! Eventually, you both might lose interest in fighting, and you might find something more pleasant to do, like going to the movies. While fighting, try to be patient with her emotions, let her express herself, and **listen**. If she really thinks she is right, let her experience the consequences of her actions and then, days later, in a quiet moment, calmly explain to her how things could have been different. **(Bronxism: it's better to let her *come to her senses* than to *knock her senseless*—and you don't have to go to jail for spousal abuse.)**

Since I turned fifty last month, I told my wife, Lourdes, that I would keep a log of all our inane arguments and include some of them in my book. Here is the only fight that survived her edit. When I turned fifty, I told my beautiful, fifty-three-and-three-quarters-year-old wife that I would dedicate the next fifty years, if I have them, to keeping her beautiful. I continued, "I plan to stay by your side even if you grow old and go dumb, like the woman in that nauseating chick flick *The Notebook*. I will protect you and provide for you. I will reduce the stress in your life. I will love you as Christ loved the church, and he *died* for the church." I thought I was scoring points, but no.

She scowled at me and rebuked, "First of all, I'm not old. Second of all, I've always been beautiful without any help of yours." (I thought to myself, *Yeah, thanks to all of that makeup.*) She continued, "And if you want to slim down and become beautiful like me, you should stop eating pizza!" (My mind drifted to Arthur Avenue in the Bronx, where they make *the best* pizza.) When my attention returned, my wife was taunting both my book and my fatness by singing the teapot song: "I'm a little teapot, short and stout; here is my handle, and here is my spout."

Isn't love just grand? Ten hours later, she asked a loaded question: "Why did you tell your readers my age?"

But my lovely wife and I will never get a divorce; I even put all of our stuff in her name just to prove that I mean to stay with her forever. My possessions would be meaningless if I lost her. Without my wife it would seem as if I had lost my whole world. I even wrote her a poem called "No Life."

No Life

I love my wife,

I love my life,

And always remember,

There's no life, without my wife.

CHAPTER 7

Albert Einstein Meets the Christian Author C. S. Lewis (Atheist Meets Believer)

Albert Einstein was not a spiritual man, but he was a great thinker and problem solver. In chapter 2, I asked a question of my atheist readers: "Would you rather be held up by a gangster who is an atheist or one who feels accountable to God?" Clint Eastwood would ask, "Do you feel lucky today?" I have yet another question for the atheists. Would you rather have Albert Einstein—a nuclear physicist, the one who discovered nuclear fission and the atomic bomb—be an atheist or be the one who feels accountable to God? After the atomic bombs were dropped on Japan, Einstein visited the devastation caused by his invention. When his plane touched down in Hiroshima, he was still an atheist, but accounts have it that when he got off the plane, Einstein fell to his knees and prayed to God for forgiveness. It was too late. Atheism is a belief system that shuns all accountability to an omnipotent God. **(Bronxism: you can run, but you cannot hide from God; and your arms are too short to go boxing with God.)**

Einstein said, "A problem cannot be solved at the same level that it was created—it can only be solved by looking down at the problem from a higher level." Put another way, a question cannot be answered out of the same knowledge base from which it was proposed. To find the answer, we must be able to transcend the thought process that created the question.

The only way we can answer the question, "Does God exist?" is if we have the mind of God. Human intellect cannot prove or disprove God's existence, because God is too large to put into a box. You cannot understand the greater God through the lesser human mind, "for the wisdom of this world is foolishness in God's sight" (1 Corinthians 3:19). Our minds have circuitry that is too puny to handle the surge of power that would be required to know God. Can a string of transistors, which is what the early computers were made of, handle the problem solving capacity of a modern *Intel processor*? God wants to reveal Himself to us, but He doesn't want to fry our circuitry during the encounter. In the Old Testament, when Moses pleaded for God to reveal Himself, God instructed Moses to hide himself in a crevasse so he could get a glimpse of God's backside as He passed by—the implication being that seeing God in His full glory would have probably blinded Moses.

Aside from a lack of intellectual power to answer the God question, we simply don't have the time to wait for an answer. We waste our time if we worship a fictional god; but if God really exists and we wait for proof before we start to worship Him, then we miss the boat to paradise.

Did you know that glass is a liquid? To prove that glass is a flowing liquid, you would have to observe a pane of glass for more than three hundred years to see that it is thinner at the top of the pane than it is at the bottom. Science takes a long time. The greatest minds who study astrophysics cannot derive one set of rules that explain observations in both micro- and macro-physics. During the past two hundred years, physicists have written a list of questions that needed to be answered before there could be a unifying theory describing our universe. Answers to one of the questions on this long list come once in twenty or forty years. Several generations of physicists will come and go, and we probably still won't be able to explain our universe, much less the existence or nonexistence of God. Is there a faster way for us to know if God exists?

Although our minds are *too frail* and *too slow* to know Him, God has bestowed an even higher power upon us—our *hearts*. The author C. S.

Lewis began his literary career as an atheist, but he tells of an enlightening motorcycle ride in which he mounted the motorcycle as an atheist, but by the time he dismounted, he was a believer in God. Something inexplicable must have happened to him in a very short period of time. In less than twenty minutes, without any rational thought, C. S. Lewis knew the existence of God. A similar epiphany must have happened to the apostle Paul when he met Jesus Christ while traveling on the road to Damascus. Before Paul became a Christian, he was a terrorist against Christianity, feeding many Christians to the lions.

C. S. Lewis and the apostle Paul were not *converted* to Christianity through their minds, but rather through a *transformational* change in their hearts, which suddenly allowed them to connect with God. The circuitries of their hearts were upgraded to a better *processor* such that it became possible for them to know God. God became real to them *instantaneously* in their hearts; the only purpose of their intellects was to help them share their experiences with the rest of the world through their books. We do not come to know God through anyone's convincing, or through mental gymnastics. Rather, it is God's grace that changes our hearts, then our nature changes, and lastly, after repeated application of the new truth in our lives, our minds are changed. Luke 10:27 describes the same transformative order by which someone comes to know God: "Love thy Lord with all thy heart, soul (i.e., nature), strength (i.e., behavior), and mind."

Do you believe that the brain is the only organ capable of having a memory or thinking process? Consider this: the heart is not merely a muscle; it is an organ full of neuropeptides and neurotransmitters. These same chemicals are found in the brain flowing through our neurons and account for our thoughts. Consider the memory of the heart through this true account. A young girl became a heart donor after been brutally murdered. The police could not find the killer until they listened to evidence that came through the nightmares of the child who had received the transplanted heart. The evidence from the living child who possessed the transplanted heart was very specific; she gave the circumstances of the murder and the identity of the killer. Modern medicine has only recently discovered some of the heart's secrets.

When an atheist speaks, have you ever noticed how complicated, circular, and convoluted his or her arguments can be? The atheist stands for the nonexistence of God. In other words, atheists stand for nothing. **(Bronxism: if you don't stand for something, you'll fall for anything.)** They reject the notion that the simplest truths are also the deepest. It is as if intellectuals can only solve the question of God's existence. God is not bigoted against stupid people; the simple man has the same opportunity to know God as does the intellectual man. Fortunately, God wants us all to know Him, the stupid and the smart. He is not playing hide-and-seek with us. His only requirement is that we approach Him as King David did, with a "broken and contrite heart." In Jeremiah 33:3, God advises the prophet Jeremiah, "Cry out to me and I will answer you and tell you great and unsearchable things that you do not know." To paraphrase, God was asking the prophet to show some desperate emotion toward God, and in return, God would give answers to questions that the prophet did not even have the wisdom to ask.

Humility is the first step to knowing God, and this concept is not limited just to Christianity. There is an Islamic saying that a man is closest to God when he bows down in prostration, because in this position, the heart is higher than the brain. The brain is useful for our day-to-day operations, but the heart addresses our eternal concerns. Rationality is the child of the mind; revelation is the child of the heart.

If humility is the first step toward knowing God, then love is the second step. In 1 John 4:8, it is written, "God is love." This doesn't mean that God is some gooey, mushy, lump of emotion, it means that God can only be known through a heart that has forgotten arrogance and has turned to loving God. Why did God send Jesus to the world as a baby? Why didn't God beam down some Napoleonic figure in the prime of his life? God was making an understatement when He sent a baby to live and love among us. He didn't want to conquer us; instead, He sent someone so irresistible that we could not help but love him. God was teaching us that love is a subtle process.

Man has never ceased in his attempts to describe love—mountains of poems and love songs have been written—but intellect cannot describe love, just as it cannot describe God. *Both God and love must be experienced firsthand.* Einstein's requisite would show us that the knowledge of love, and the knowledge of God, comes only at the high level of the heart, which is higher than the intellect. The scripture, in 1 John 4:7, goes on to say, "Everyone who loves, has been born of God and knows God. Whoever does not love, does not know God."

CHAPTER 8

East Meets West (Islam Meets Judeo-Christianity)

The photograph at the beginning of this chapter is that of St. Mary Magdalene Russian Orthodox Church, Jerusalem, Israel. Notice how the architecture combines both Muslim and Christian elements, particularly the minarets topped with crosses. I once dreamed I was standing between two rails of a railroad track that stretched into the farthest horizon. A fire had broken out in front of me, and flames were consuming the rails. As I witnessed the rails gradually melting, I felt sad and hollow. I wanted to be on the train that used those tracks, but now my journey had ended because of the flames. The two rails in my dream represented my dilemma: I was trying to decide between Christianity and Islam—the fire, satanic fire—was separating and destroying everything that should be together. Satan is our common enemy. My purpose is to show that Christians and Muslims have more things in common, if only through our shared stupidity, than we have reasons to drift apart. Only by the love of God can we mend the tracks and get back on our journey. God is most interested in how we conduct ourselves during the journey; He does not care about our destination, because for the real seeker (he who is thirsty for the tea), God will eventually reveal Himself—provided that we follow God's plan for our salvation (the tea is thirsty for you).

It is tempting to be politically correct by exercising tolerance and saying that all religions lead to God. Perhaps we could create the best monotheistic religion on earth if we combined *the great traditions* of Judaism with *the love* of Christianity and *the discipline* of Islam. But what was God's Plan? In all three monotheistic religions blood must be spilled to avert God's wrath against our sin. Jews and Muslims sacrifice lambs and goats on a yearly basis for the atonement of sin. For Christians it is no longer necessary to spill the blood of animals because Jesus was the sacrificial lamb who was slain, once and for all, for the atonement of man's sin, past, present, and future. Isaiah 53:5-7 describes the sacrifice of Jesus, "But he was pierced for our transgressions, he was crushed for our iniquities; the punishment that brought us peace was upon him, and by his wounds we are healed … he was led like a lamb to the slaughter."

Throughout history, man has tried to reach up to God by practicing a myriad of religions, but in only one instance did God reach down to man through the sacrifice of Jesus Christ. Muslims have an entire chapter about Jesus in the Koran, Jews have prophesies pertaining to the coming of Jesus, their often forgotten Messiah, in the Old Testament. It is written in John 3:16-17, "For God so loved the world that He gave his one and only son, that whoever believes in him shall not perish but have eternal life. For God did not send his son into the world to condemn the world, but to save the world through him." *It was God's plan to unleash His wrath, and the wrath of Satan, and the agony of all human sin on Jesus.* All of this suffering was triangulated onto the cross of Jesus Christ in accordance with God's plan. Isaiah 53:10 says, "Yet it was the Lord's will to crush him and cause him to suffer, and though the Lord makes his life a guilt offering, the will of the Lord will prosper in his hand."

God has a plan to free us from sin, thus perfecting our hearts, so that He can receive us with His perfect love. It is good news that God had a plan for the atonement of our sins; the literal meaning of the "Gospel" is "good news." All we have to do to receive the Gospel is to humbly acknowledge that we are sinners who are in need of a savior who was elected by God, and whose name is Jesus Christ. Jesus said of himself, in John 14:6-7, "I am the way and the truth and the life. No one comes to the Father except through me. If you really knew me, you would know my Father as well." For myself, and probably many other Muslims who became "closet Christians," the earliest encounter with Jesus was very brief, we may not have even known it was him, but the encounter was life-changing. I started out seeking Allah (the Arabic word for God), and then Allah gave me Jesus with the Gospel as "good news" for my life. All along, with His infinite wisdom and mercy, God had the perfect plan for me.

How can it be so easy to receive salvation through the Gospel? It is easy because God never intended for even one of us to go to hell. Hell was not primarily created for humans; hell was made to punish Satan, and for Satan's legion of fallen angels, and for arrogant men who refuse God's free and munificent help. For the humble seeker of God it is easy to receive Jesus when he appears to us in a dream or a vision. Loving Jesus comes naturally to everyone because God created a place in our hearts for the one who spilled his own blood to fulfill God's plan for our salvation.

The lights of the world grow strangely dim as we love and follow Jesus, and the light of God's glory glows more and more brilliantly in our deeds and in our faith. The burdens of life seem lighter once we surrender to the will of God. Even death loses its bite after we are free of the consequence of sin and become reconciled with God's love. At the moment of death, the believer is showered with God's love and peace, as seen in the accounts of near-death survivors (see chapter 4). On the Day of Judgment, all believers, from all time, will collectively get caught up in the rapture of God's love.

I have just painted a picture of the ideal Christian life as God had planned it; but institutionalized Christianity has much to be desired. Although Groucho Marx once said, "I would never join a club that would have me as a member," we need to attend church precisely because none of us are worthy enough to stand before God on our own merit. Mahatma Gandhi was the leader of the Indian independence movement of the early twentieth century. As a young man, Gandhi tried to visit a Christian church, but the ushers told him, "This is a 'whites only' church, so get out." If those ushers had not been racists, then all of India might have been Christian. Later in his life Gandhi said, "If Christians aimed to be more like Jesus, then the whole world would become Christian; the message of Christ is so beautiful, too bad it has to be evangelized on the lips of Christians who do not seek to be like Jesus."

Where was the love? The Book of Revelation is full of rebuke for churches that have lost their original love for God. Revelation 2:4 states, "I hold this against you, you have forsaken the love you had at first." Many modern churches lose sight of the most important biblical principle, that of love. The devil is in the details for those serving in church ministries. Performing good work in a ministry puts you on Satan's radar screen. Church ministries can easily become self-serving "mine"-istries, where the emphasis is on the work of man rather than on the love of God.

The love of God is the highest priority. God comes first, followed by the love between husband and wife; followed by the love between parents and their children; followed by the love between brothers and sisters; followed by the love for extended family, friends, and neighbors. The Bible advises us not to bring an offering to the altar before first making amends with our brother. People should not light a candle in the church before they light a candle in their home; they should not be permitted to serve in a ministry without first being on good terms with their God and with their families.

Some Christians will dilute the principles of the Bible into a more convenient, politicized form. For example, a church that has dispensed with the fifth commandment (honor your parents) to avoid losing popularity with youngsters in the youth ministry. When conflicts happen within families who have hormonally challenged teenagers, it is expected that the church be a part of the solution, not a part of the problem. What is right is not always popular with teenagers. What is popular is not always right. Therefore, churches should not seek to be popular, but in all things they should seek what is right in the eyes of God. The rules of the church should never supersede the commandments of God.

God warns the church of Laodicea about becoming a church of expediency in Revelation 3:16: "So, because you are lukewarm—neither hot nor cold—I am about to spit you out of my mouth." Jesus angrily toppled the tables of the money changers at the temple. What would Jesus do with churches that pander to modern-day money changers through the occasional Ponzi scheme? The Bible says, "Judgment begins in the house of the Lord." Christians should show more respect for the Bible, and they should take a page from Muslims who vehemently defend the Koran (hence the fatwa of death to anyone who denigrates the Koran).

We cannot look at people as models for Christ, because no imperfect person or imperfect church can represent Christ perfectly. Instead, we have to focus on the Bible for Christ's examples of perfection and righteousness. My wife and I have moved to a much smaller Assembly of God–endorsed church. We are blessed by our new church, because it has made a pact with other like churches to follow biblical principles. Many times throughout human history, man has tried to reach up to God through man-made religion, but in only one instance did God reach down to man with His own plan for our salvation through the sacrifice of Jesus Christ. That is why I want only Christ, not the man-made institution of religion.

History tells us that Jesus had a very unnatural way to fight a battle. He did not rely on the strength of His own arm, He would pray for His enemies, He never lifted a finger to defend Himself or His religion, and His weapon of choice was the wooden cross upon which He was crucified. (See the short story later in this chapter, titled "The Torn Page.") The Christian crusades were political battles fought by warmongers who, like the Muslim fundamentalists, pretended to wage holy war for God's glory but really had other motives. To the real Christian, the term *holy war* is an oxymoron. Jesus had no use for battles against fleshly enemies. Jesus prayed for His tormentors even as He was on the cross. He did not hold His tormentors responsible, for He knew that the real battle was against Satan. Ephesians 6:12 tells us that "our struggle is not against flesh and blood, but against the spiritual forces of evil in the heavenly realms."

History tells us that Muhammad fought many battles to ensure the viability of his new religion. Muhammad was a prophet, a statesman, and a soldier. He was born through natural childbirth, and he never claimed to have any miraculous powers. In the Koran, Sura 17 (Al-Isra), verse 93, Muhammad describes himself: "Am I aught but a man—a messenger?" In the Hadiths (sayings of Muhammad), it is written that Muhammad would repent of his sins seventy-two times each day. What does the Koran say about Jesus? My Muslim mother taught me that you couldn't be a Muslim if you didn't believe in what the Koran said about Jesus and his miracles. My advice to the fundamentalist Muslims, who wish to kill Christians for a supposed jihad, is to study what the Koran has to say about Jesus, "the prophet of love." The Koran acknowledges all the miracles of Jesus Christ, including his virgin birth. In Sura 19, verse 19, the Koran calls Jesus, "A man without fault."

The Koran says, "If a man kills another, then it is as if he has killed all humanity; and if a man saves another's life, then it is as if he has saved the whole world." That is a beautiful scripture, but there are also scriptures in the Koran that pertain to war and killing. War was a fact of life during early Islam. The dawn of Islam was a tumultuous time, and war would rage between rival Arab tribes. In modern times, the battles against non-Muslim Arab tribes have been replaced by a battle against Christians and Jews. Although most Muslims are peaceful, a fanatical few have interpreted the language in the Koran as a command to kill the kafirs (kafir means infidel or unbeliever, or someone who does not believe in one God and the Day of Judgment):

- Sura 33 (Al Ahzab), verse 61: They shall have a curse on them: wherever they are found, they shall be seized and slain without mercy.
- Sura 9 (Al Tawbah), verse 29: Slay those who believe in neither Allah nor the last day.
- Sura 22 (Al Hajj), verse 39: To those against whom war is made, permission is given to slay, because they are wronged and verily Allah is most powerful for your aid.

The fundamentalist Muslim's war against Christians and Jews is misguided. Christians and Jews *are believers* in one God and the Day of Judgment; they are not atheists or polytheists. When I was a small boy, my mother taught me about jihad. She described it as the unseen battle we fight every day, men and women, against Satan who seeks to rule our minds and our hearts. This sounds remarkably similar to the battle that

Christians fight when they "put on the armor of God" against Satan in the Bible—Ephesians, chapter 6. After the terrorist attack on 9/11/01, a Muslim television commentator debated the question of the salvation of a suicide hijacker: "Does he go to heaven or to hell? The Koran says that anyone who commits suicide will go to hell, but the Koran also condones jihad, or holy war, as one of the five pillars of Islam. Anyone who dies in a holy war will die a martyr."

I remember wishing I could reach into the television and slap this man's head. Of course, the hijacker goes to hell, because his jihad is misdirected and he has killed innocent people, not because he has committed suicide!

Atheists will say that this terrorist attack proves that God does not exist. A good God would not have permitted this attack if He really existed. What is the answer? First, God honors the free will of man, including the terrorist's will to bring death and destruction.

Second, God has allowed Satan to have temporary dominion over the earth. Revelation 12:12 proclaims, "woe to the earth and sea, because the devil has gone down to you! He is filled with fury, because he knows that his time is short." The terrorists who attacked America have prostituted themselves to Satan, but rest assured, God can take the most horrific deed spawned by Satan, turn it upside down, and use it to destroy the forces of evil from within. God uses evil to cannibalize evil; this is as true for the terrorist as it is for the crack cocaine addict. The very people opposed to God are used as tools to execute God's will. Revelation 17:8–17 says, "The beast and the ten horns you saw will hate the prostitute; they will bring her to ruin and leave her naked; they will eat her flesh and burn her with fire. For God has put it into their hearts to accomplish His purpose by agreeing to give the beast their power to rule, until God's words are fulfilled."

Third, God permitted this attack to draw Americans to seek him— persecution strengthens the church. Christianity in America has never been confronted with persecution until now. The apostle Paul writes in 2 Corinthians 12:10, "That is why, for Christ's sake, I delight in weakness, in insults, in hardships, in persecutions, in difficulties. For when I am weak, then I am strong, because God's power is made perfect in weakness."

Ask any persecuted Christian missionary serving around the world, and he will say, "In the moment of our greatest suffering, we develop clarity to our vision so that we can plainly see God." Strangely, it seems that God is closest to us when we are in despair with our backs up against a wall. Sometimes we even have to suffer at the hands of mortals to feel the fullness of God's presence: *with great burden comes greater love.* God's love never forsakes us. Survivors of 9/11 saw visions of Jesus in the stairwell, and as a sign of His presence, there were the amazing steel girders fashioned into a cross by the intense heat from the fires.

I was once just a Muslim from Pakistan, but after 9/11, I am also a Christian from Manhattan Island. I pray that God will invert the original purpose of this satanic terrorist attack, and as such, God will bring more people to become seekers of His love. When times are good, we Americans think that our success is because of our own wisdom and might. Persecution from fundamentalist Muslims reminds us that we are still vulnerable and need to turn to God for protection and answers. Furthermore, we need to pray for those who persecute us, just as Jesus prayed for his tormentors when He was on the cross. Despite 9/11, if we are motivated to pray and practice fasting, Americans can regain their spiritual center of gravity, and many more Muslims can encounter the precious love of Jesus Christ.

This book contains the account of three Muslims, one gangster, one crack addict, and one Orthodox Jew, all of whom found the love of Jesus. Here is a story of a soldier from Afghanistan who drove a tank during the Russian occupation. We Americans are the next superpower in Afghanistan, but I wonder what weapon Jesus would use to win the hearts of the citizens there. Would he use a tomahawk missile or a drone plane, or would He use his old standard weapon, the wooden cross?

I briefly met this Afghani man in New Jersey. One may ask what a New Yorker was doing in New Jersey. I was at a Jesus for Muslims conference. The man (whose name escapes me) and I exchanged stories about how we came to know Jesus. I remember thinking, *I hope they don't deport this guy back to Afghanistan, because the state department might think he's a terrorist.*

My story is in chapter 4; here is his story.

The Torn Page

I was walking out of a teahouse in a small village where I used to live in Afghanistan. Suddenly a man bumped into me, and he silently stuffed something into my shirt pocket before he hurriedly walked away. From the size and texture of what he had deposited, I could tell it was paper, but I dared not remove it in public. On the way home, I thought the paper could be from a Russian spy; maybe the Russians wanted me to switch sides. I'd never do it!

When I got home, I locked the door and made sure that I was alone before I pulled the paper out of my pocket. It was worse than I had suspected. This was a half-torn page from the Bible, and on the top, it had someone's name on it: Matthew. I read it carefully, because there may have been a message in a secret code. The page had a scripture on it: Matthew 5:44: "Jesus said, Love your enemies, and pray for those who persecute you, that you may be sons of your Father in heaven."

First, I made sure that there was not any code, and then I started laughing aloud, thinking, *those crazy Christians! Don't they know you need guns and bombs to fight the enemy? Why would anyone ever pray for his enemies?* Although I got a good laugh and did not take this advice seriously, I kept this torn page from the Bible in a small pocket in my military uniform. To this day, I don't know what moved me to keep that slip of paper.

Days passed, weeks passed, months passed, and we kept fighting the Russians. I slowly became obsessed with the idea of loving my enemy. Every night before I went to sleep, I would take out the half-torn page from the book of Matthew. I needed to find someone who knew what it meant. A man from Iran lived nearby, and rumor had it he was a Christian. Tomorrow morning, I would go and ask him to explain what the scripture meant.

The next day, I walked to this man's house and made sure no one was following me. He was an older fellow, and seemed the kind who didn't care about anything and didn't fear anything. I say this because on the wall of his living room, for everyone to see, was the cross of the Christians. I hurried to pull out the half-torn page from the book of Matthew. I didn't want to be in his house for too long, as I felt it was not safe.

The man only needed a quick glance at the paper for him to know what it was. Then, with a warm smile that beamed with joy and recognition, he asked, "What took you so long to come?"

Then I placed his face with that of the man who originally stuffed the paper in my shirt pocket at the teahouse. It was him. At first, I was fearful for myself and for the old Christian lunatic who tears up Bibles and stuffs them in the shirts of Afghani soldiers. Who is next to walk through the door? Maybe it will be my commander!

I felt drawn to this man. There was something inviting about his old face, a face with wrinkles where years of smiles had been. His eyes were bright with joy and fatherly love. I felt a strange peace in his presence, though I knew we were in wartime Afghanistan. This old goat could easily get us killed; nevertheless, I needed to get him to explain the words on the page—his Bible, his torn page, his inconsistent idea of loving one's enemy.

His explanation came very slowly, despite my efforts to speed him up. He said, "Muhammad had a sword, Bin Laden has a machine gun, Jesus had a cross. Three soldiers with three different weapons. Who do you think will win a man's heart?"

I thought about what he had said and answered, "You cannot beat someone into loving you. If you did, the love would be very superficial, and it would not be real love."

The man was delighted at my answer. "Yes! Yes! Now, who do you think is your real enemy? The Russians whom you have been killing, or is it Satan who causes you to hate the Russians?"

I was just beginning to understand, when suddenly the joy drained from the man's face. "It is very dangerous for you to be here. The authorities are coming any day now to apprehend me for my Christianity. I have a contact in Iran whom I want you to meet. He will take you to America. I'll write down for you this information. You must go before it is too late; God be with you."

A part of me did not want to go. I did not want to leave this lovely old man alone. A part of me wanted to stay and die with him. I loved him as though he was my father. I was trying to decide what to do. Judging from the old man's great love and his great courage, I knew he wouldn't permit me to stay, even though I was not afraid. After all, I was a soldier, but for which war? Then it dawned on me, I had been fighting the wrong war, against the wrong enemy!

"You must go now. God be with you, my brother in Christ," the old man said.

When he called me his brother in Christ, it was as if he was looking into my soul. I started to feel I was a Christian. I could feel the love of God. I knew that God had planned for me to succeed this old man and his dream. Maybe he'd had this plan for many months, or even years. How did this old man know my motives and me? How did he know I would do what he said? Why do I trust this old man so much? Why do I love him?

I thought if this was his last wish before the authorities got to him, then I knew the old man could be trusted. A man who was staring death in the eye had no reason to lie. I would take him up on his offer, and besides, I really wanted to go to America and see Madonna, the Material Girl.

I took the paper with the contact information and turned, ready to leave. The old man stopped me and said, "Wait. Take my cross." I placed the cross in the secret pocket of my uniform along with the torn page from the Bible. I have kept these items for many years to remind me of my first Christian teacher.

The next day, I packed a few choice belongings for my trip to America through Iran, but I wanted to see my old friend one last time. When I got to his home, I noticed the outside walls covered with blood and machine gun fire. A tear welled in my eye, but I immediately put a halt to my emotions. My mind remained sharp. I dared not publicly grieve for my friend. I dared not go inside his house. I kept walking until it was safe. I asked a young boy playing in the street if he knew what had happened to the old man.

My fears were confirmed. The boy told me the authorities got him last night. "Last night?" I asked. "What time last night?" The boy started laughing, and then with a devilish grin said, "Soon after you left. Ha, ha, ha!"

Fear and anxiety welled up inside me. My heart started to race as I looked around to see if anyone was listening. I reached for some chocolate in my pocket to give the boy for a bribe. "Here, now don't tell anyone. You hear? Don't tell."

The chocolate seemed to turn him temporarily back into a young boy, as only moments ago he appeared to be a demon. I did not wait for the boy's answer. Instead, without actually running, I walked away as fast as I could. I did not want to appear conspicuous. I made it to Iran, found my Christian contact, and by the grace of God, here I stand before you—a Christian in America!

Apologetics toward Muslims

Muslims understand and agree with two-thirds of the Trinity: Father God and the Holy Spirit (to Muslims the Holy Spirit is called Barak, which can be roughly translated as "the grace of God," which incidentally is our current US president's first name), but Muslims have a problem when Christians call Jesus the son of God. There is no disrespect intended for Jesus, who Muslims see as a prophet, but they believe that God is too high and mighty to be associated with an equal, or with a son, because it would take away from the majesty of God. Other problems Muslims have with Christian theology are accepting that Jesus was an atoning sacrifice for the sins of all humanity, misunderstanding that Jesus sought equality with God, and accepting the Trinity. In the next few paragraphs, let me take a shot at answering these Islamic concerns about Jesus.

Christians call Jesus the son of God. But what do you call someone who was born of a virgin as orchestrated by God? The only other people who were not born of a woman were Adam and Eve. What was the difference between Adam and Eve and Jesus? Adam and Eve were the only people created without belly buttons; they were not born of a woman. If Adam and Eve were the two naughty people who ushered in the original sin for all humanity, then why is it so hard to believe that one man, Jesus, could take the garbage of all humanity out? I take out the garbage in my house. My wife sends me out in the middle of the night with the garbage, because she does not want the children, or herself, to be eaten by a bear or a wolf. Out of my abounding love for her and our children, I risk my life every time I take out the garbage. **(Bronxism: garbage removal is risky business—just go to New York and ask the Mob.)** God's plan was for us to transform our human nature to become more like His nature, so He could love us perfectly, but sin got in the way. God's Holy Spirit cannot do its transformative work on a dirty, sinful heart. Enter Jesus, to remove our sin and give us a clean slate with God.

What about the Muslim's concept of obtaining salvation through good works? Aren't there heavenly scales that weigh a man's good deeds against his bad deeds? We cannot pull ourselves up by our own bootstraps. In the Koran it is written that if we all got what we deserved, then *"Allah would not leave a single human standing on the back of the earth."* It is only by God's grace, and His plan, that we go to heaven—not by our good works. If God gave us salvation according to our works, then no one would go to heaven. The Bible says that humankind's best works are "but filthy rags to God." In Ephesians 2:3–10, it is written: "We were by nature objects of wrath … God made us alive with Christ even when we were dead in transgression. For it is by Grace you have been saved, through faith—and this is not from yourselves, it is a gift of God—not by works, so that no one can boast. For we are God's workmanship, created in Christ Jesus to do good works, which God prepared in advance for us to do."

The Christian does good works out of the joy of serving God, not because salvation depends on these works. Does this mean that the Christian can go on sinning now that Christ has already paid the penalty for everyone's sin? Absolutely not. God's salvation through Jesus Christ is unconditional, but God's promises are conditional. Although the gift of eternal life is offered to anyone who believes the Gospel of Jesus Christ, we still bear earthly consequences for the evil that we do. Sin separates us from God's promises of "Love, power, and soundness of mind" (2 Timothy 1:6).

What is this Trinity? Jesus was the culmination of God's plan to teach us through an example of perfect human nature. As a bonus, the sacrifice of Jesus absolves us of our sin, paving the way so that God's Holy Spirit could start working to purify our nature until it becomes one with God's nature (upon which God has brewed the perfect cup of tea). There are three players in the plan to make perfection out of our sinful human nature: God, Jesus, and the Holy Spirit. All are from God; all are three aspects of the same plan. I've heard an analogy that helps describe the Trinity. The sun is one object, yet it has three perspectives that we can appreciate: heat, light, and mass. Another analogy: a person is one being, yet he can have three names—a first name, a middle name, a last name.

The mystery is that these three entities (God the Father, Jesus, and the Holy Spirit) are separate, and at the same time, they are the same. If we contemplate the moment before Christ's death, we get a unique opportunity to study the integral parts of the Holy Trinity. In his life, Jesus performed miracles by the Holy Spirit; in his death, the Holy Spirit resurrected him. Christ himself asked of God, "Father, why hast thou forsaken me?" (Matthew 27:45). At that moment, Christ was, for the first time ever, feeling abandoned by God the Father and the Holy Spirit. This separation was in preparation for Christ to take on the burden of humanity's sin; Christ had to suffer crucifixion as a human, alone, and unassisted by the Holy Spirit. When Christ was close to death, he called out to God the Father and the Holy Spirit, "It is finished" (John 19:30), and once again, God's love in Christ was made powerful as the Holy Spirit lifted Christ out of his grave. God's love is subtle, and it has its own logic. God's love does not conquer us, but it is meek. Love is vulnerable, unless the Holy Spirit assists it, just as Jesus on the cross was vulnerable when he was separated from the Holy Spirit. Christ's body was in a state of ruin before the Holy Spirit lifted him; herein lies a lesson for all of us who find our own lives in ruin. In the moment of our greatest suffering, the Holy Spirit is closest to us, but too often, we are unaware of its presence. In Romans 8:11 it is written: "He who raised Christ from the dead will also give life to your mortal bodies through His Spirit, who lives in you."

The politician defines greatness as someone who has many people serving him. Jesus defines greatness as someone who serves many people. In Matthew 20:28, Jesus says, "whoever wants to become great among you must be your servant, and whoever wants to be first must be your slave—just as the Son of Man did not come to be served, but to serve, and to give his life as a ransom for many."

Here is another example of the servitude of Jesus Christ: John 13:1–15: "Jesus knew that the time had come for him to leave this world ... Having loved his own (disciples) who were in the world, he now showed them the full extent of his love ... so he got up from the meal, took off his outer clothing, and wrapped a towel around his waist ... and began to wash his disciples' feet, drying them with the towel that was wrapped around him. When he had finished washing their feet, he asked them, 'Do you understand what I have done for you? You call me Teacher and Lord, and rightly so, for that is what I am. Now that I, your Lord and Teacher, have washed your feet, you also should wash one another's feet. I have set you an example that you should do as I have done for you ... Now that you know these things, you will be blessed if you do them."

Out of His abounding love, God wanted to know us more passionately than we could ever want to know Him (the tea was thirsty for us). What is even more overwhelming is that God sought a relationship with us, by Himself becoming like us, through the flesh and blood of Jesus Christ. Jesus walked among us. We can call him our brother, we can call him our example, and we can call him our savior, because he took the hit on our behalf. Did Jesus think he was an equal to God, or equal to the Holy Spirit? Not at all. In Philippians 2:5–8, there is a description of the humility of Jesus: "Your attitude should be the same as Jesus Christ who, being in very nature God, did not consider equality with God something to be grasped, but made himself nothing, taking the very nature of a servant, being made in human likeness. And being found in appearance as a man, he humbled himself and became obedient to death—even death on a cross!"

If any of you Christians out there are planning to minister to Muslims, here's a synopsis of my advice:

Ministering to Muslims

✓ Ask if they believe that it is only through **God's grace** that we are saved, for in the Koran it is written that if we all got what we deserved, then **"Allah would not leave a single human standing** *on the back of the earth." God chooses us* to be saved—we don't deserve to be saved because of our works.

✓ Ask if they believe in the *miracles of Jesus.* The Koran has an entire chapter on Jesus—on his virgin birth, on how he breathed life into a clay bird, etc. Adam and Eve created the original sin for all mankind. It is not so far-fetched for a Muslim to believe that Jesus could, by God's power, be resurrected from the dead and carry out God's plan for the salvation of mankind.

✓ Ask if they have ever seen Jesus in a *dream or vision.* There are many closet-Christians among the Muslim people. I was one.

✓ And most importantly, ask if you can *pray with them!* Prayer will melt your hearts together, and all boundaries between you will dissolve!

CHAPTER 9

The Yankees Meet the Mets (No Contest)

This is a short chapter.

The Bronx rocks!

The Yankees rock!

The Mets stink.

No contest.

CHAPTER 10

Old Meets Young (Raising a Child)

The greatest Japanese attack on America since Pearl Harbor has been through the invention of video games. Japanese kids grow smarter by programming these video games, while American kids grow dumber by playing them. What is worse, these games leave our kids with a false sense of accomplishment, as if they did something for their bodies and their minds. I am not suggesting that our kids should get a rubber ball and a broomstick and play stickball in the street, as I did. I am not suggesting that they read a book, as I did, and I am not suggesting that they talk to people, maybe even people of the opposite sex, as I did. All I am saying is that modern children require instant gratification, there is no time for reflection, and they lack perspective. When I was a young man, my best friend and I created a two-part greeting that replaced saying "Hi, how are you?" This greeting reminded us that wisdom is a lifelong pursuit. One of us would say, "Be content with less," and the other would reply, "Remember, you'll be an old man one day."

There are many holes in a modern kid's life when it comes to things like teamwork, accountability, fairness, morality, and empathy. Video games, however, do prepare the young adult for the rat race. This is the rat race: you work hard to get your stuff, you work hard to keep your stuff, and all the while, others are working hard to take your stuff away. *Rat Race* would make a great title for a video game.

One hundred years ago, when life expectancy was forty-five years, a child would be emotionally mature by the age of fourteen or fifteen. Today, with the life expectancy of eighty or more years, children do not mature until the age of twenty-five or thirty. Maybe it is because people are living longer, but it seems our kids are precocious when it comes to running the rat race, and yet, they are emotionally immature when it comes to relationships. Do not stop parenting just because your teenagers are not in diapers anymore. Teenagers need parental guidance to help them get through their emotional roller coaster of the hormonal years. Teenagers need parental wisdom to help counteract their gonadal thinking. Unfortunately, the media portrays parents, especially fathers, as being clueless and irresponsible. And who wants to listen to parents when everything a young adult needs to know can be Googled and then practiced on a video game? There is a saying, "Hire a teenager before they find out that they don't know everything!" Maybe all that hormonally driven bravado is worth something. Mark Twain had this description of himself when he was a teenager:

When I was a boy of fourteen, my father was so ignorant; I could hardly stand to have the old man around. But when I got to be twenty-one, I was astonished at how much the old man had learned!
—Mark Twain

The Bible says, "Spare the rod and you will spoil the child." I think spanking is counterproductive after the age of five or six, but parents need to set some kind of boundaries on any child living under their roof. Privileges should be taken away whenever those boundaries are crossed. An Islamic proverb teaches, "A child is to be treated like a king until the age of seven; for the next seven years he is taught how to be a slave; and for the next seven years he is taught how and when to serve, and how to graciously accept being served." If all else fails, then leave your kids to their own devices, let them have kids of their own, and let those kids "do unto them as they did unto you," in a sort of reverse Golden Rule. One of my pharmaceutical representatives, a woman in her late twenties, told me that she called her mom to apologize for all the heartache she had caused her mother through the years. What prompted this apology? The young woman had a fifteen-year-old daughter of her own who was giving her grief. Here is a poem about teaching a child, from the child's perspective, written by my friend's son:

Teach Me Well

Tell me and I'll forget,

Show me and I might remember,

Involve me, come along side of me with love,

not above me, and I'll understand.

Generation X, a group born after the baby boomers, wants what they want, and they want it now. They will dispense with teamwork, accountability, fairness, morality, and empathy just to get what they want. Somewhere along the way, kids should learn to do good for others, as it helps build relationships with those whom they serve. Jesus called that the Golden Rule. But Generation X wants to be rich at the price of being emotionally poor, and they are in a hurry to achieve their goal. My advice to kids of Generation X is this: take it slow. Sit down with a parent and sip a cup of monkey-picked, oolong tea. Good kids should not be in a rush to become bad teenagers; good teenagers should not be in a rush to be bad adults; good adults should not be in a rush to be bad spouses; good spouses should not be in a rush to be bad parents. **(Bronxism: learn how to drive fifty-five in the slow lane, rather than seventy-five in the fast lane. You'll get there two minutes later, but at least you'll be in one piece.)**

When your kids are clamoring for freedom, tell them to "Be careful what you ask for, because you might just get it." Being a grown-up is no fun. Freedom does not mean that you are a master of your destiny, or that you get to do what you want, when you want. Freedom does not mean getting rid of someone's influence in your life. Freedom does not depend on your circumstances; you can be free in a jail or you can be a prisoner in a mansion. Are children free when they are allowed to hang out all night on a street corner, or are they just neglected by their parents?

Ask your kids, "What do you need to be free from?" The best answer would be, "I need freedom from myself." We must learn at an early age to be other-centered, not self-centered. The freest person is someone who serves others and expects nothing in return. Freedom from the self means that you learn to anticipate the needs of others, even before your own needs are met. If others depend on you, and not the other way around, then you are free of needing them. The freest thing children can do is to keep their elderly parents in their home instead of putting them in a nursing home. Freedom means having greater responsibility.

Besides freedom from the self, what else should we be free from? We should be free from impulsive behavior, the opinions of people, the need to acquire a great many things, and stupidity. *Self-restraint* means that no one can make you mad, because you are in charge of your emotions, and no one can fight you, because you will not enter into someone's boxing ring. *Contentment* means that you are happy with what you have. The lights of the world grow strangely dim as the light of God grows brighter in your life. Things seem much less significant, your desires change, your attitude changes, your demons leave you, you lose your addictions, and you stop being ruled by things that you thought you needed. *Joy in your life* is not determined by your circumstances, or by what others think of you; your joy comes from feeling that God is always near. Your *purpose in life* is simple, it is to obey God and serve humanity. **(Bronxism: one plus God is always a majority.)** Lastly, we must be *free of stupidity*. In the Old Testament book of Hosea, the prophet Hosea laments, "My people die from lack of Knowledge." A proverb in the New Testament reads, "The wise man foresees trouble and hides himself." **(Bronxism: wise is the person who knows what to say and when to say it, but even a fool appears wise until he opens his mouth to speak.)**

We can strive for freedom from self, the opinion of people, material things, our circumstances, and our stupidity, but we cannot be *free of sin* by our own merit. We are not righteous enough to stand sinless before God. Sin prevents us from being close to God. God Himself bridged the gap caused by our sin so that we may have a close relationship with Him. God offered up His only son, who was free of sin as a lamb for sacrifice, so that the rest of us could avoid the slaughterhouse for our sins. The apostle Paul tells us, "Jesus made me free from the law that brings sin and death" (Romans 8:2). The Law of Moses cited the criteria for our sins, but the New Covenant (Jeremiah 31:31) spares us from eternal death from sin, because Jesus nailed the ordinances of the law to his cross. That is not to say that Christians can be lawless. If we continue to sin after what Jesus has done, it is as if we are asking Jesus to go back on that cross.

It is hard to convince rebellious, hormonally challenged, young adults how to conduct their lives. Children throughout the ages have sought freedom from the values of their parents as if they could reinvent a better wheel. Freedom from one's parents means nothing when a child remains a slave to sin. In every revolutionary movement, another, sometimes worse dictator, replaces the previous dictator. "The parentless child will have Satan as a guide," according to an Islamic proverb. Preparing children to find God's purpose in their life requires teaching them to be free from self, the opinion of people, things, and circumstances; dependency on all of the above leads to a life of slavery and sin. According to the Bible, "The wages of sin lead to death." Sin crushes the human spirit to the point where we cannot approach God. God's ultimate purpose for us is to "brew the perfect cup of tea." This happens when our human spirit, no longer tainted by sin, mingles with God's perfect Holy Spirit. It is through freedom from sin that we can enjoy a relationship with God, and our lives become joyous with all the privileges and purposes that God intended for us, His children. **(Bronxism: happiness is short lived, and it depends on happenings. Joy is forever, and it depends on feeling close to God.)**

When a man's body is in relationship with God, *he is at peace*; when his soul is in relationship with God, *he experiences joy*; when his spirit is in relationship with God, *he is holy*, and his life is set apart for God.

Thoughts about Honoring One's Parents

Parents know about life; they have been there, done that. Parents have solutions, but who wants to listen? Children will not listen, because they are not yet mature; they are sheltered from the harsh realities of life, and they can't handle the truth. Despite their lack of experience, children think that they already know it all! Worse than that, some children want to claim they are mature and independent but they are still on their parents' dime!

Kids will treat their friends, and even parents of their friends, better than they will treat their own parents! As we grow older, God grants us a way for us to better tolerate the younger generation. God mercifully reduces our senses, so we don't see and hear the younger generation. Alzheimer's disease is just an old person's way of telling young people that they aren't important enough to even think about!

The Koran says, "Heaven is at the feet of mothers." A Jewish mother's curse says, "May you have a child that puts you through the same trouble that you put me through!" What does the Bible say? God wants us to honor our parents in a manner that mirrors our relationship with the Almighty. Adults should seek a relationship with God, just as children should seek a relationship with their parents. Respect for parental authority learned as a child should teach us how to seek God when we are adults.

As adults, we are to fear God in a manner that parallels how a child is to fear his parents. Of course, it is better to love and respect God, but because human nature is weak, we often have to fall back on fear to establish a correct relationship with God. The Bible says, "The fear of God is the beginning of wisdom." **(Bronxism: people turn to God more often because they feel the heat, not because they see the light.)** If, as parents, we can't be loved, then we should be respected. If we can't be respected, then it is necessary that we be feared. Whether parents are loved, respected, or feared, children need to honor their parents, as per the fifth commandment.

The fifth commandment is the only commandment with a promise: *a promise* of long life and prosperity for those who follow it. The corollary to the fifth commandment, for those who dishonor their parents, is *the curse* of a short and unsuccessful life. The wrath of God is real. As Christians, the blood of Christ saves us, but there are still consequences to our actions.

How does the fifth commandment help us with modern parenting issues? Even the least wise of parents can teach their children through example of what not to do, but rebellious youths would rather make their own mistakes than learn from the mistakes of others. A child who refuses to absorb his parents' wisdom will lose at least a decade of his life because of his poor choices. The good things in life will come much later, if at all. Blessings will be fewer, and life will become more difficult and more dangerous. The lost decade can be from lost length of life, or it can be from a lost quality of life. Poor choices made early in life greatly diminish the likelihood for success later in life.

Children who don't honor their parents mature very slowly. They seek coddling even as they rebel. They must be victimized by life before they can learn from other people's mistakes. Worse still, these children, when they grow older, lack the behavioral template to have an edifying relationship with God. They never fulfill the plan that God made for their lives, a plan to prosper them and give them a purpose. Why do you think God calls himself, "Father" God? It is because God wants us to honor our parents in a manner that mirrors our relationship with the Almighty God.

Our relationship with God sets the standard for all our other relationships. If we do not seek God, we will look for love in all the wrong places. We will destroy worthwhile relationships (such as that with our parents) over some unimportant conflict. With the passage of time, conflicts grow deeper. If you put a bad relationship on a shelf, don't expect it to get any better when you finally come around to deal with it. You will have cold spells in your relationships, but be like the fleeting ice on a lake, not like a glacier in Alaska. Why is the ice so thick in Alaska, yet it is thin where it covers a lake? The conditions in Alaska enable ice to grow thick: everlasting cold, months without sunshine, unforgiving winds, never a hope for a warm season to thaw the mile-deep ice. The closer you are to God's love, warmth, and light, the better you will thaw out and resolve your conflicts.

My wife was thirty-two when she gave birth to my daughter. Unfortunately, that birthday aligned her menopause with my daughter's premenstrual syndrome and my sleep apnea/narcolepsy. Although I slept through most of their quarrels, I remember having a sinking feeling. Back then, I would describe myself as a sinking island of testosterone in a sea of estrogen (or lack thereof). My daughter wrote this about her mother on an application to Bible College.

We Have Bumped Heads

The most influential person in my life has been my mother. My relationship with my mother is very important to me. Although we may bump heads at times, she and I have always had a special connection in which we genuinely care for each other. I can truly tell that she wishes the best for me in all aspects of my life. My mother has taught me many things, and I admire her for that. Before attending preschool, my mother taught me how to read. At an early age, I fell in love with books. My mother has always pushed me to achieve academic success; I recall the many workbooks she would assign me during the summer break: reading, writing, and mathematics. She also enrolled me in Kumon for four years, which is a learning center that establishes math and reading skills. My mother created a strong foundation for academic performance in all of her children.

I recall the words in her prayer: "Lord, I plead the blood of Jesus on Sabina's life, around her, above her, beneath her, and between her. I believe she is protected by the Blood of the Lamb ..." Through this prayer, I felt protected and blessed.

My mother also encouraged me, at an early age, to read my Bible and to pray habitually. Looking back now, I know that this has contributed to the kind of relationship I now have with the Lord. I have learned more and more the importance of spending time with God, and learning of His Will for my life. In addition, I can clearly remember the times when my mom would pray over me and my brothers before we slept; she would always play Christian music in the car and at home. Little things like this have stuck in my memory and have influenced me. I remember listening to her prayers and the lyrics of the songs; I would ponder the meaning and then ask my mom for an interpretation, which she graciously would give. I remember one particular worship song that went, "I will worship you God until the very end ..." But I told my mother that there is no end to worship, because we worship God on earth while we live, and then in heaven when we die. I am thankful for my mother and all of the things she has done, because she has shaped not only my study habits, but also my relationship with God.

What is the difference between a wife and a daughter? My daughter, Sabina, used to see my fat belly and poor fashion sense as a positive thing. My daughter, when she was eight years old, told me, "Daddy, never get thin, because your jelly belly makes a perfect pillow for watching television." She would even play a game with me called "guess how many M&Ms can fit into Daddy's belly button." We had two versions of the game, plain and peanut. If she guessed right, her prize was to eat the M&Ms! Once she asked me, "Daddy, why do you have to go away to these Christian men's retreats? I don't want you to go!"

I asked her, "When you fall asleep on the sofa, who carries you to your bed?"

She answered, "Why, you do, Daddy."

I continued, "And when Daddy falls asleep on the sofa, who carries Daddy?"

Her eyes grew wide. "Nobody, you're too big and heavy!"

"That's why I go away on retreats, because when Daddy grows weak and tired, I need God to lift me up and carry me."

Here is a poem about me by Sabina, age eight, which is remarkably insightful and is true even today.

My Daddy

Sweet, spiritual, strong, strict.

Father of Sabina.

Lover of Food, Family, Knicks.

Who feels Lovable, Special, Comfortable.

Who needs Clothes, Knicks Tickets, Exercise.

Who fears losing his Family, Dying, losing Me.

Who gives Kisses, Hugs, Cuddles.

Who would like to see a Good Report Card, Heaven, Me.

I call him Daddy.

The following dramatic story has appeared, with some variation, in the Torah, the Bible (Old Testament), and the Koran. My parents retold the story and commentary to me.

The River of God's Mercy

The mother of Moses was terrified at the possibility of her son being killed on the orders of the Pharaoh. Being a pious woman, she pleaded to God for help. In the version from the Koran, God said this to her in a revelation while she was praying: "I have chosen your son Moses to be a messenger and a prophet. Do not fear or grieve, because your son will be safe, and after a short time away from your son, you will again give suckle to him." If God had stopped there, I am sure Moses's mother would have been delighted, but God needed to test her faith. God continued, "If you fear Pharaoh and want my help, you must build a cradle for your baby out of reeds, and you must cast Moses into the river." Imagine her horror, but she was a woman of great faith, and she did what God had advised.

As the story goes, Pharaoh's wife plucked Moses out of the river. She wished to raise him as her own son, to which Pharaoh agreed, but the baby required a wet nurse. Through a series of complex events, it was none other than the biological mother of Moses who was chosen to suckle her own son. God was in control of the destiny of Moses. A praying mother cried out for divine intervention in a seemingly impossible situation, and God did things for her son that were greater than she could have ever imagined. As an infant, Moses became the adopted son of the very tyrant who had designed a plan to kill the leader of the Jews. Who had the better plan: God or Pharaoh? God used this little insignificant boy, in his mother's flimsy cradle of reeds, as His instrument to unravel the Pharaoh's empire, because eventually, Moses emancipated the enslaved Jews. The atheist is like Pharaoh, who believed it was possible to create a better plan than God's plan. Intellectual arrogance is a great sin, and it ultimately causes us great suffering. The Koran puts it very plainly: "Surely we belong to God, and to Him we will return."

Not too many mothers would make a cradle of reeds for their children, even if that were all that God required. Jewish mothers—and all mothers in general—are guilty of worrying too much for their children. They need to pray more, and they need more faith in God. (**Bronxism: if you pray, why worry; if you worry, why pray?**) All God expects from us as parents is this: prayer, faith, and a flimsy cradle of reeds for the baby Moses, or a feed trough in a manger for the baby Jesus. The baby Muhammad was an orphan; he too had a humble beginning. It is God who does the heavy lifting and the most intricate planning, confounding the naysayers. Glorify God's name, and in time, He will exalt you and your purpose in life. There is no greater purpose for a parent than to protect and provide for one's children, but realize that God is in control. Giving up the illusion of control and self-direction means to let go and let God. Sometimes we have to cast our children into the River of God's Mercy.

Everything in creation belongs to God, including what we think to be our intellect, power, and strength. Belief in one's self, rather than in God, prevents us from ever discovering what God had planned for our lives. What if the mother of Moses tried to outsmart Pharaoh and sought to hide her baby? She was not smarter than Pharaoh and was definitely not smarter than God. She made the right choice, putting her baby in God's hands, and the Jews had a leader to take them out of Egypt.

CHAPTER 11

Health Meets Sickness
(A Tribute to My Mother, a Cancer Survivor)

As a doctor, I have been around more than my fair share of sickness and death. Life must be very precious, because everyone who is approaching the end of life always wants to stay alive just a little bit longer. But is the hereafter a better place than this world? An Islamic proverb says, "Yes, it is, because newborn babies cry when they get here, and old people have a serene look of peace when they leave."

I almost lost my mother to ovarian cancer in 2001. I can recall that while she was ill, I held my mother's life as more precious than my own; a loved one's life is very, very, precious. My mother had people from every religion, culture, and creed praying for her during her illness. Doctors told her she had only a few months to live, but God had another plan for her. Nine years later, she is a miraculous survivor of stage four ovarian cancer. The following is a story that celebrates precious love for Grandma and Grandpa, written by my son Rasoul when he was about twelve.

The Tallest Little Man

My grandfather (better known as Papa) is the tallest little man I know. At five feet four inches, he towers above just about everything that's little. This includes young children, small animals, most furniture, and my pocket-sized grandma (better known as Amma), who just barely scrapes the five-foot mark if she stands on her toes. For anyone under the category of "people who make Papa look big," Papa's receding hairline was no issue. In fact, for all the tiny people he knew, he might have had a pink mohawk studded with Christmas lights. They couldn't see his hair or care less about it. But for all of us giant monstrosities, who measure past the five foot, six-inch mark, we could all see that Papa was losing his hard-fought battle against the imminent threat of balding.

I had never thought hair was that important to my grandpa, but apparently, it was. Week after week, we'd watch Papa try something new in hopes of hiding the soon-to-be-barren wasteland he called a scalp. He tried everything, from gel (which I believe is supposed to make your hair look thicker), to hats (which of course he couldn't wear in the house). Week by week, we all saw a steady stream of different hair products/supplements find their way onto my grandpa's head. Still without luck, he went to the classic "comb-over," but it truly looked like a lost cause. In my opinion the "comb-over" had to be the saddest attempt; yet, of course, I didn't say anything, because that would just break my poor grandpa's heart. He who had fought so valiantly against the inexorable beast that is a receding hair line. I remember thinking to myself while looking at my grandpa's brown scalp through a wide-meshed net of gray hair, *I wish I could give Papa some hair. I get self-conscious just looking at him.*

Months passed, and the "comb-over" still remained surprisingly unchanged over the last few months, but it was no longer the focal point of attention. For you see, it was during this time that my grandmother had tested positive for ovarian cancer. She was to undergo several operations and many weeks of chemotherapy. There was so much more than grief in my Papa's eyes—eyes that trembled like the smile underneath it. And strangely enough, my grandma found strength in that quivering smile with eyes to match, enough strength to get through many different procedures and weeks of chemotherapy that would leave her debilitated for some time.

As you may know, chemotherapy comes with a high cost. Many people become extremely ill while going through it, and hair loss is to be expected. My grandma was no exception. Within weeks, my grandmother's hair was completely gone, eyebrows, eyelashes, the whole nine yards. Embarrassed, she would put on her dupatta (a traditional Indian veil) before leaving the house to cover her bare head. My grandpa just couldn't bear to see his wife in such dismay. So one day he had a brilliant idea.

Papa waited for Amma to leave the house. Then, once he was sure she was gone, he proceeded to the bathroom, where he took a razor and shaved every last bit of valued hair he had left. He shaved his head right down to the scalp—not even a trace of the thin gray hair remained; it was absolutely bare, like a shining, yummy, malted milk ball. When Amma came home, she was overwhelmed by what my grandpa had done. There stood Papa in the doorway, crouched low enough so Amma could get a perfect view of his yummy, chocolate-tootsie-pop of a head. And, like a dam had broken, tears rushed out of Amma's eyes, and between sobs, she just laughed and assailed Papa with butterfly kisses. All he could do was laugh. I don't even think he heard his wife saying, "I love you," because their laughing was so loud. And the smile, which now seemed engraved in my grandpa's face, looked perfect under eyes that glimmered, and a bald head that shined.

Love is something that you do to show someone you care. It's about willingness to give up part of yourself to fill the emptiness in other people. This idea encompasses every type of love you can imagine, from romantic love to a family/friend type of love. It's a concept that I'm learning to live by, it is an idea that I try to keep at the core of my being, and this unselfishness guides my actions. And hey, maybe one day, I'll grow as tall as my grandfather when he bends down and lets his wife touch a head that he shaved for her.

My Dog Seth

St. Francis of Assisi once said, "Minister at all times, and only sometimes use words." St. Francis must have known my dog, Seth. Seth has only one word, "Woof." Yet, his example of love and loyalty goes beyond that of any person I know. Some of you might be thinking, "What's that dog doing with a Jewish person's name?" Seth is not a dog—he is a furry, four-legged person. His previous owner named him, and I did not want to confuse the dog by calling him Snowball.

Seth is an American-Eskimo breed, and I got him from an American-Eskimo rescue foundation. My brother-in-law brought Seth to our house hoping that my family would fall in love with him. His owner, who was suffering from terminal cancer, sent a folder containing the dog's vaccination information. I told my wife to figure out some excuse to tell the kids why we could not keep Seth, as we already had a dog. As I was talking to my wife, Seth was sniffing the folder from his master. He had recognized his master's scent. I picked up the folder and started thumbing through the pages. Seth followed the folder to my hand, sniffed it wildly, and even tried to bite it out of my hand. It was then that I realized he was a very loyal dog. I told my wife that I had changed my mind—we could keep him. I could not let such a loyal creature be euthanized. The kids were overjoyed, but my wife could not figure out why I had changed my mind so quickly. Later I told her, "I married you pretty quickly too, didn't I? It was love at first bite."

Fast forward to 2009—this was probably the worst year of my life. I was diagnosed with a severe case of sleep apnea. During the sleep study, I found out that for a minute at a time, I would stop breathing in my sleep. During these apneic periods, my oxygenation would drop to 50 percent, and my heart rate would fall to twenty-nine beats per minute. The sleep lab technologist said he almost called for an ambulance five times over the course of the night when he monitored my sleep. That explained why he would frequently come in to wake me up. I got angry with him after the fifth time he woke me. I said, "Hey, man, don't wake me! I was dreaming that I was flipping burgers, and just when you woke me, I was about to take a bite from a cheeseburger!"

The technologist said, "Cheeseburgers are bad for you. If I had waited for you to eat that cheeseburger in your dream, you would have died from the cholesterol!"

I was worried that my severe case of sleep apnea was a ticking time bomb. My wife started sleeping in the other room because my loud snoring kept her awake, but my dog, Seth, never left the foot of my bed. For a long time, I wondered why Seth frequently barked in the middle of the night, as there seemed to be no reason. Then it suddenly hit me—Seth was barking every time I stopped breathing in my sleep—he was saving my life at least five times per night, and I had only saved his life once. Since then, I've had surgery for my condition, I've lost twenty-five pounds, and now I have only mild sleep apnea. I still snore, though not as loud. My dog, Seth, still watches over me at night. Seth is my guardian angel at the foot of my bed.

The Hem of His Robe

This story is about an Iranian Muslim man named Parviz, who was a friend of my Christian brother, Manny. You will recall (see chapter 4) that Manny was the Cuban brother who showed me that I needed Christ's love and saving grace. Parviz and Manny worked as engineers for the New York City Mass Transit Association. They would frequently converse, comparing Christianity with Islam—always in a way that respected each other's holy books and beliefs.

One sad day, Parviz found out he had inoperable pancreatic cancer and had only a few months to live. I never actually met Parviz; we were supposed to get together through Manny, but his death intervened.

I wept for Parviz, not because he died, but because Manny had only spent one year teaching him about Jesus. On the other hand, I have known Manny and the love of Jesus for twelve years. I really felt bad for Parviz, as if he had been cheated. Parviz's life was shortchanged on earth, but not in heaven, as I later found out from Manny. Parviz could sense his time was short, and from what he had learned about the Bible from Manny, he wanted to "touch the hem of the robe of Jesus," for healing. Although

God chose not to heal Parviz's body, God healed Parviz's spirit through a dream in which Parviz encountered Jesus. In this dream, Jesus laid a hand on Parviz's shoulder, and then Parviz fell to his knees and wept from joy, because God's love overwhelmed him. The next morning, Parviz said he felt a wonderful peace wash over his entire being.

In the remaining few months of his life, Parviz would telephone Manny and ask him for prayers. Manny, who is always there for a friend, graciously prayed with Parviz. Parviz's newfound love of Jesus bolstered his prayers, although he never formally accepted Christ as his personal savior. Parviz continued to pray like a Muslim on a prayer mat. God could hear Parviz when he prayed; God knew his broken and contrite heart.

Parviz had a hobby of carving beautiful wooden bowls. He finished his most significant carving just weeks before he died, and then he went to heaven. Here in his own words is a description of his Jesus Christ Bowl.

The Jesus Christ Bowl

I began working on this particular wooden bowl in the spring of last year. I found a broken tree in front of my work building and decided to use the wood from it. This particular kind of wood is called *honey locust*. Later, I decided to look for the same type of tree in the park on Randall's Island. I discovered a tree that appeared to be the same as the honey locust, but I saw that this tree had thorns. When I reached out to take a sample of the thorns, one of them pricked my finger, and it was extremely painful. I wanted to know more about this type of thorn, so I decided to search it on the Internet. What I found was that these thorns are named *Jesus's Crown of Thorns*. Since Jesus's message was to give love, and he suffered through great pains to give love, I decided to attach those thorns around the bowl that I created. On the top of every thorn, I placed a heart-shaped leaf that I had carved, which represented the heart of Jesus. In addition, I turned ebony wood into a morning glory flower to represent God's glory, and I carved a butterfly to represent the freedom that we receive through Christ's love.

—Parviz, July 23, 2010

CHAPTER 12

Turning Fifty Meets Fear of Dysfunctional Relationships, Loss of Purpose, Insignificance, and Dying

I turned fifty in October of 2010. I wrote this book between Thanksgiving and Christmas, and I hope my readers appreciate the hemorrhoids I have suffered. I am in a rush to write this book about strained relationships, because I am afraid that I might die before it's finished, and that not all these people will reconcile! I sound like one of the neurotic characters from the Woody Allen movie *Annie Hall*. Here is a vignette from *Annie Hall*. Two brothers go into a psychiatrist's office to get help for their dysfunctional relationship. The older brother complains, "Doc, you gotta help my little brother, he thinks he is a chicken!" The psychiatrist says, "It must be very hard living with your younger brother." To which the older brother replies, "No, not really, Doc. You see, I need the eggs."

I once had an Orthodox Jewish patient, L. R., who suffered from mental illness and HIV. Here is his story.

The Mantle of Peace

One day while I was conducting the HIV clinic, I received a frantic call from L. R.'s psychiatrist, who thought either L. R. was experiencing some horrible side effect from the HIV medications, or he was on crack cocaine. I told the psychiatrist to send L. R. straight to my clinic. When L. R. got there, sure enough, he began to bother the staff, and the nurses begged me to see L. R. ahead of everyone else. Once he was in my office, my first question was whether he was under the influence of any illegal drug, to which he adamantly said no. His HIV medications could not cause such a rapid change of behavior, so I asked him to tell me honestly what was wrong, but I was not prepared for what he had to say.

It took him a while to catch his breath, because he had been crying profusely. "Today is my father's death anniversary. For nineteen years, my family would pick me up, because I don't drive, and take me to his grave, but this year no one came to get me. Then I went to my temple. I was crying for my dead father, but my tears repulsed the rabbi, and he chased me out because he didn't want my 'HIV tears' in the temple. Then I went home and found a letter from my wife on the table. She and my two sons were gone. She said she was going away with my two little sons and said that our marriage is over!"

I was taken aback, not knowing how to respond. I remember blinking, and in that fraction of a second, I pleaded with God to give me some words of healing and encouragement for this poor guy. The words that came out of my mouth were not mine. "Your father's spirit knows that it was your intention to go to honor him. It was not your fault that you were absent at his gravesite. Your rabbi kicked you out of the temple, but the real temple is in your heart, it doesn't require a building. Your sons will always be your sons forever, and one day soon, they will come back to you. All the people in your life today have let you down and made you very sad. But how would you like to know someone who will never let you down and will never forsake you?"

Drying his tears he asked, "You, doctor? Do you mean you will always be my friend?"

"Of course, I am your friend." I was choking back tears of my own. "But I can share with you a friend I have who loves us unconditionally and forever—his name is Jesus."

By now, we were both weeping uncontrollably, but this time the tears were for joy, because my Orthodox Jew patient, L. R., said, "Yes! I want a friend like Jesus to love me and to help me with all the burdens in my life!"

This entire encounter took no more than fifteen minutes, and when L. R. emerged from my room calm and smiling, blessed with the peace of God, my nurses were certain that I had administered a shot of some powerful tranquilizer while L. R. was in the room.

The story does not end there.

That weekend, I attended a Christian men's retreat, and on a Friday night at nine o'clock, I asked my brothers in Christ to pray for the sad patient of mine. Women pray all the time, but God really gets excited to hear a man pray, more so when there are one hundred men praying together! **(Bronxism: when we work, we work; when we pray, God works. Who do you think gets more work done?)**

Monday morning came around, and I was back at the clinic. Whom did I see as my first patient, full of smiles and laughter? I practically dragged L. R. into the room, because I was convinced that God had done something wonderful for him during the weekend. I said to him, "Wow, you have changed since the last time you were in my office! What happened to you?"

He began to answer, but I could not help but be distracted by something other than his words. It was the love and peace of God resting on his shoulders, the same shoulders where the burdens of his life had been. He wore God's love and peace like a warm mantle around his neck.

He spoke slowly. "It was very strange, but last Friday at nine in the evening, I got a call from Maryland, and it was my wife. She was crying, and she begged me to take her and my boys back!" That was no coincidence. The men at the retreat had been praying at that exact same time.

God obviously has a sense of humor. He brings me, a Muslim man from Pakistan, to tell another man, an Orthodox Jew, about the love of Jesus. God is not a respecter of human institutions, or religions, or socioeconomic class, or gender, or race.

We prayed the following prayer of salvation with a sense of gratitude and repentance: "Oh, God, I realize that I have not lived my life for your glory. I have been a sinner, selfish and narrow minded. I need you to guide me through difficult situations that I know will destroy me if I depend on anyone but you. Come into my life now, Lord. From this day on, I will no longer pollute my heart with selfish desires. Lord, cleanse me and make my heart a suitable vessel where the water of my life acquires the flavor of your Holy Spirit. Pour out the essence of my life into the sinless cup that is the atoning sacrifice of Jesus Christ. I long to receive the forgiveness you have made freely available to me through the sacrifice of Jesus on the cross. Lord, take pleasure when you sip from this cup, a cup that you created when you desired the loving hearts of all of your servants."

We rejoiced, and the angels rejoiced. I had nothing more to say, except "God is great!" And he said, "All the time!"

EPILOGUE

The simplest truths in life are paradoxically the most profound. The simple truth of God's unconditional love creates a dilemma for the arrogant intellectual: why is it that a simple-minded person can know God through a purified heart, while the pompous intellectual cannot know God despite all kinds of mental gymnastics? The answer is simple: the heart is the highest faculty for knowing God's love for us, not the mind. God loves all people equally, and He wants His profound love to be available to all of us, not just the intellectuals or any other supposedly "privileged" group.

The greatest human accomplishment is that of a reconciled relationship through the gift of love, even if this love was short-lived and fleeting. Shakespeare once wrote, "It is better to have loved and have lost, than to never have loved at all." But God's gift of unconditional love creates the most sublime relationship, because it lasts forever and it is never wanting, nor can it be lost. Everyone craves God's supreme love, though the atheist does not know what he is craving. All human ambition is motivated by the simple need to fill a void in our hearts, to restore a human relationship, or more fundamentally, to restore our relationship with God.

The principle of reconciliation through unconditional love holds true for all people and in all relationships. In the relationship between warring nations, this principle brings *peace*; in the relationship between squabbling family members, this principle brings *harmony*; in the relationship between a sinful individual and God, this principle brings *joy*.

Evil people throughout history have often suffered from an earlier loss of love. The Trojan war was fought over the lost love of a woman, Helen of Troy; Hitler's hatred of Jews may have stemmed from his unsuccessful courtship of his Jewish girlfriend—she rejected him and we got World War Two; Saddam Hussein's genocide of his own people may have stemmed from his mother's failed attempt to abort him—while pregnant with Saddam, his mother tried to abort him by pressing her abdomen against a stairway railing; and Muammar Gaddafi's killing of his own people may have been because he lost love for his cosmetic surgeon—Gaddafi wants to kill the plastic surgeon who botched his face-lift, and this surgeon is apparently hiding out with the rebels.

If life gives you lemons, make lemonade. Enjoy the simple things, do what you can, and do not worry about the things that you cannot change. Each day has its own cares and problems; do not worry about tomorrow's boulders while you are breaking today's rocks, and let go of yesterday's pebbles. God knows how much you can bear, that is why He has set before you this day only manageable-sized rocks. Do not imagine your rocks to be boulders. How do you know that you have been blessed? You know you have been blessed because God has held your hand while He hammered your boulders into rocks, pebbles, and even dust. God wants you to grow in faith as you labor on earth for His glory in heaven.

The Bible says that the best works of mankind are nothing but "filthy rags" to God. I should not sing my own praises, although it is only human to want to draw everyone's attention. Jesus thought I was worth dying for; my dignity and integrity lies with him. I look forward to standing before God and hearing Him say, "Well done, my good and noble servant," not because of my book or any other achievement, but because of a life spent *obeying* God while *serving* and *loving* people. I will try to be humble, and I will try to be a person who brings reconciliation. This would be better than becoming someone who boasts and brings division. Jesus said, "Blessed are the peacemakers."

We fifty-somethings have entered into a phase of life where real wealth is measured by the number of people who love us, and the amount of time we have to share with our friends and family. God is more interested in our journey and who we take along than He is in our destination. I don't know where I'm going, but I'm on my way—and I'm even making good time! But I will take time to enjoy, time to love, and time to serve while I'm getting there, and then maybe I will find my perfect teapot.

I can identify with an old cartoon and television show, *Popeye the Sailor Man*. Popeye said, "I am what I am, and that's all that I am, and I'm Popeye the Sailor Man!" Popeye did not need anyone under age thirty-five to help him define who he was, or to issue him a certificate of approval; Popeye's identity was with spinach, while my identity is with Christ. Popeye ate spinach to become *mightier*, while I sip tea to become *meeker*, because God's power in me is made perfect in my weakness (2 Corinthians 12:9). Jesus said, "The meek shall inherit the earth."

Life is short, but it is wide—there are many opportunities, many places to go, and many people to see. This is the secret of life: learn what God's purpose is in your life, learn what strengths God has given you, learn what human need you are to fill, and then apply yourself. Don't be like the theologian—the more he knows, the less he applies. The theologian will go into a fine restaurant, and because he loves words so much, he is content to eat the menu. Life is for living; do not read about it, or watch it on television, or simulate it on a video game.

When we are young, we feel we are so important, so indispensable, and so invincible, but the world goes on without us after we grow old and die. If we want to make a dent in history, we have to stick to the purpose that God has ordained for our lives. I will always take solace in knowing that the will of God never leads you to a place where the grace of God can't keep you. I have come to terms with my own mortality only because death is part of God's plan. No one lives forever.

At the end of life, what do we value most? No one cries out from his or her deathbed for a gold watch or the deed to his or her property; instead, people call out to their loved ones and their God. They seek the touch of an understanding hand, a final kiss, and they seek to put a halt to the pain of this world. A legacy of love and reconciliation is the most wonderful memory that we can leave our loved ones when we die. Ask yourself, are you the kind of person who *sheds the light* of love, faith, and hope? Or are you the kind of person who *casts the shadow* of bitterness, doubt, and guilt?

My cousin Javid is fifty-six years old. The last fun thing Javid did was to spend a weekend camping with his extended family. Then on the following Monday, he had a heart attack, and then on Tuesday, he had a stroke. But even as he is recovering, he has never stopped celebrating life with his loved ones. He continuously sheds light, he is never bitter, and he never casts shadows.

We still go camping with Javid, only now we camp out in the waiting room behind the intensive care unit and in the cafeteria of the hospital. We bring our own home-cooked meals, play games, try to tilt the vending machine, and tell jokes. We have everything but the campfire! I told Javid that he has to get better by next summer so that he can once again lead us on another camping trip. Our extended family hasn't missed a beat. This is how we celebrate Javid's life: we live, we love, and we take care of one another. Through our love for one another, we are reconciled with Javid's new health issues. Far from being a negative, Javid's illness has brought us all closer to one another and closer to God.

One day, we will all go to that final campground in the sky, but until then, I will only spend time with the people who want to spend time with me. There's no sense being around mean people who judge you. The people who judge you don't matter and the people who matter don't judge. Instead, the people who matter will shower you with *the gift of unconditional love.* This unconditional love entices us to seek an even greater love: God's *perfect love.* Through our troubles and suffering, God permits the water of life to come to a boil, and the Holy Spirit provides the tea leaves with which we are to flavor our lives. When the tea is brewed and ready, God Himself will pour the perfect tea from the perfect teapot, into the sinless cup—the cup is the sacrifice of Jesus. Then, finally, the seeker sips the tea, and the tea sips the seeker.

Habib Ibrahim opened the first HIV clinic in Rockland County, New York, in 1991. In 2005, he opened an HIV clinic in the Bronx, New York City, and has treated HIV for over twenty years. Dr. Ibrahim lives in New York with his wife and three children.